THE

# BIRD
# FEEDER

G U I D E

HOW TO ATTRACT
AND IDENTIFY
BIRDS IN YOUR
GARDEN

# BIRD FEEDER

## GUIDE

### HOW TO ATTRACT AND IDENTIFY BIRDS IN YOUR GARDEN

MARCUS SCHNECK

DORSET PRESS
NEW YORK

DEDICATION

*To my mother, who gave me a love for birds*

A QUINTET BOOK

This edition published 1989 by
Dorset Press, a division of Marboro Books
Corporation.

ISBN 0-88029-367-5

This book was designed and produced by
Quintet Publishing Limited
6 Blundell Street
London N7 9BH

Creative Director: Peter Bridgewater
Designer: Terry Jeavons
Project Editor: Judith Simons
Editor: Patricia Bayer
Picture Research: Marcus Schneck

Typeset in Great Britain by
Text Filmsetters, London
Manufactured in Hong Kong by Regent Publishing
Services Limited
Printed in Hong Kong by South Sea Int'l Press Ltd

# Contents

# Introduction

OPPOSITE A red-bellied
woodpecker gorges itself on
an abundant supply of late-
summer berries.

MIXED AMONG my childhood memories is the recurring image of a mockingbird that seemed ever present in the backyard. The specific, individual bird changed every few years, as a new feathered occupant drove off his predecessor. But the solitary figure was always there, eager to defend its territory against all comers. Once perceived as a trespasser, no creature was immune to the bird's fury, not the battle-ready blue jays, not our overweight beagle, not any member of the family. The ancient cherry tree with its abundant summer fruit, the favored perch on the peak of the shed roof, the thorny barberry hedgerow with its red berries and thorn-protected nesting cover, the suet feeder, were all property of the mockingbird.

Each spring and summer, the bird would attract a mate and raise an offspring or two from a nest in the barberry. By the time the autumn frosts were heavy on the lawn, however, all family ties were voided. After a few days of chasing about the property, the lord and master was again the lone mockingbird. My mother maintained a running contest with the bird, trying to whistle, squeak or otherwise produce some sound that the bird could not mock. The mockingbird was generally up to her challenge, as well as that of mimicking the dozens of other bird species that frequented the bird feeders. Some of them never seemed to see the humor in it, attacking the mocker in a flurry of feathers.

My earliest memory of the birds is now more than two decades old. My mother, who was the birdwatcher/bird benefactor in the family at the time, is no longer with us. But one of that original mocker's successors still lords over the backyard. For me, that living mockingbird memory mingled with special thoughts of my mother is more than enough reason to continue backyard habitats wherever I live.

Other reasons abound for taking the time, trouble and expense that most certainly goes into a full-range backyard program of habitat development and supplemental feeding.

**ABOVE A birdwatcher lives here. All the gear needed for hours of enjoyment awaits the next feathery visitor to the backyard.**

For those practical thinkers, birds destroy an immeasurable number of insects every year, preventing damages estimated in the hundreds of millions of dollars. Likewise, North America would be awash in a sea of thistle, ragweed, dandelion and similar weeds if not for the thousands of tons of seeds that the birds eat annually.

On a less practical, but equally valuable, level, birds are the splash of color across the gray winter landscape, the melody of a hundred voices on a spring morning, the unsteady hop of a speckle-breasted baby robin on the heels of a parent stalking worms. They are the insight gained into the private lives of wild things over years of observation.

For all of this, the birds require only the four basic requirements of survival: a year-round supply of food, a constant source of water, shelter from enemies and the elements, and protected spots for nesting and rearing their young. They won't even demand that all four be provided in the same backyard. Somewhere within the neighborhood, somewhere within the area that they acknowledge as their territory will do just fine. Of course, the backyard that does provide all four in one convenient location will be blessed several times over. The birds provide their services in proportion to how well their needs are met. Backyards and gardens – and their owners – that offer all four at peak capacities will gain most from the birds.

This book aims to help anyone with a backyard or garden, even a deck or a patio, to achieve one of those inviting spots of habitat that will draw birds like a magnet. Whether the property owner is starting from scratch with a freshly planted new lawn around a newly built home or a jungle-like tangle of trees, vines and ground cover about a 200-year-old farmhouse, there are ideas and techniques here to make that spot more attractive to birds.

The benefits for man and bird alike are tremendous, particularly in this age of rapid habitat loss, when every square foot saved is critical.

ABOVE Residents of this home will soon be treated to a front-row seat to view the beginning of life for some young starlings.

PREVIOUS PAGE Invite the birds into your backyard and they'll share the intimacies of their lives with you.

ABOVE During the winter months, a well-stocked bird feeder will draw color and life into the backyard.

ABOVE Backyard birds, such
as the tree swallow seen here,
also "pay" for what they're
offered in seed and habitat by
eating large quantities of
harmful insects.

# 1

## Feeding and feeders

OPPOSITE Mesh bags can be used to hang suet in the backyard, however they tend to wear out quickly under the heavy use that suet attracts.

13

FROM THE first human to drop some of his meal on the ground outside his hut and see birds pecking at the scraps, man has probably been a bird feeder. Of course, in those earlier times, when the struggle for survival was a full-time occupation, motives were less altruistic than today. Birds visiting the feeding site could be the next meal.

Bird feeding as we know it today, however, really began in the 1950s. The growth of the activity has been phenomenal. An estimated one in three North American families puts out an average 60 pounds of seed each year. They spend an estimated $500 million annually.

The benefits attributed to all this vary with the expert making the calculations. Nothing drastic would happen to the bird population if the supplemental feeding was stopped, according to some. Local populations could decline, say others. Recent range expansion of species such as the mockingbird, northern cardinal and house finch could be reversed, according to a growing body of evidence.

There is no argument that individual birds that otherwise would not survive harsh winters are pulled through by the artificial food supply. After a heavy snowfall or ice storm, every feeder visitor – and there will be many – is helped through a particularly rough period.

Traditionally bird feeding has been associated with the winter months. Local flocks of birds do come to rely on a particular feeder for at least part of their daily diet, and cutting off the food supply could mean death for some. At this time of year, a bird's survival is a matter of finding enough food every day to keep its metabolic rate high enough to generate sufficient body warmth. Crucial feeding times are first thing in the morning, after a night of burning calories to keep warm on roost, and last thing in the afternoon, just before entering another long cold night on roost.

While bird feeding remains vastly a winter activity, a growing number of feeders now get their first loads of seed in early fall. Their owners have discovered that at this time of

**ABOVE Birds are just as satisfied taking their seed from a homemade feeder cut from a plastic bottle as from expensive, commercially produced feeders.**

year birds are establishing their winter territories and a regular, reliable source of food will encourage them to remain in the vicinity. Feeding has also extended much later into spring and summer.

Many backyard feeders are now filled year-round. This often brings normally hidden activities, such as courtship and breeding, into view. And, many parent birds will later bring their fledglings along to the feeders. In mild weather, of course, when there is plenty of wild food, birds will make less use of feeders.

Which species you attract at any time of the year is determined by three factors: the species that make their homes in your region, the foods you offer and the way you offer them.

The first is the most easily understood and agreed upon. Obviously, the ruby-throated hummingbird won't visit a Nevada backyard, no matter how many tubes of sugar water are offered. The bird simply does not live in that part of the United States.

The second factor is debated as much as the benefits of backyard feeding. It is impossible to create one seed mix that will draw birds better than all others in every locale. The blend of bird species is too variable across the entire North American continent. Even from neighborhood to neighborhood in the same town backyard feeders often see a different mix of visitors.

ABOVE Bird seed comes in
many shapes and sizes. From
left, white proso millet, niger
seed, cracked corn, oil-type
sunflower and peanut hearts.

As a result, every feeding enthusiast, nature center and wildlife sanctuary touts a special blend of seed above all others. "Recipes" fill the pages of many books on the subject. Much of the advice and debate is based upon individual observations of birds at feeders, and the seed mixtures generally do work very well in the locales where they are recommended.

## The Geis study

Researchers have adopted the same tact, but with much larger databases, resulting in more widely useful recommendations. A landmark study was conducted by Aelred D. Geis of the U.S. Fish and Wildlife Service and a horde of volunteer observers in California, Maine, Maryland and Ohio. Through hundreds of thousands of feeders they determined which seeds some common birds preferred. The seeds and the birds that showed first preference for them were:

Black-stripe sunflower seeds: common grackle; hulled sunflower seeds: American goldfinch, white-crowned sparrow; peanut kernels: blue jay, tufted titmouse, white-throated sparrow; oil-type sunflower seeds: chickadees, evening grosbeak, mourning dove, northern cardinal, purple finch; red proso millet: mourning dove; white proso millet: brown-headed cowbird, house finch, mourning dove.

ABOVE The northern cardinal
puts its well-adapted bill to
good use on oil-type sunflower
seeds.

Second preferences were: black-stripe sunflower seeds: blue jay, chickadees, evening grosbeak, northern cardinal, purple finch, tufted titmouse; golden millet: house finch; hulled sunflower seeds: common grackle, white-throated sparrow; niger seeds: American goldfinch; red proso millet: brown-headed cowbird.

The study also found several ingredients, commonly used in commercially available wild bird mixes, to have essentially no attraction for their intended diners. They were hulled oats, milo, peanut hearts, rice and wheat. Mixes including these will cost more in unwanted items in the bird feeder and waste when most birds reject them.

ABOVE A testing tray feeder
will help determine the seed
preferences of visiting birds.

Geis observers used experimental, segmented feeders in their study. An easy-to-build "testing tray" will allow you to make similar notes, specific to your backyard.

Any compartmentalized, wooden tray will do. The one I've used for a few years is made of ⅜-inch plywood. It's 18 inches long by 3 inches wide by 1¼ inches deep and divided into six equal compartments by 1¼-inch-high walls of the same wood. A flat, 18-by-6-inch roof 12 inches above the tray offers some protection from wet weather.

In testing different seeds on my local birds, I may fill each of the six compartments with a different type of seed or three compartments with one type of seed and the other three with another variety.

Obviously, such small compartments do not hold enough seed to keep even a small flock of birds satisfied for very long. The testing tray is not meant to be a feeder, but a means to learn what the birds want me to put into the regular feeders around the yard. A half-hour of observations during the peak morning feeding sessions, another half-hour sometime during the day and a half-hour during the evening peak for several days soon begin to show a trend in the seed preferences of the birds.

A flock of American goldfinches might empty half the supply of niger seeds on each visit, while a few evening grosbeaks might clean up every last oil-type sunflower seed every time they stop by. The white proso millet compartment might be untouched by both groups.

## Ringing the dinner bell, just right

Put out the right food and you will undoubtedly attract birds. Put out the right food in the right way and you will attract many more.

Mourning doves prefer to feed at or near the ground. Pine siskins love clinging to hanging feeders or trays, eating their fill over relatively long periods of time. Chickadees visit both types of feeders, but prefer to take one seed at a time to a nearby perch rather than eating at the feeder. Diversity will attract all three species, and many others with their own special preferences.

A highly successful blend of feeders includes a hanging or pole feeder filled with sunflower seeds, a hanging niger seed feeder, a ground or tray feeder filled with cracked corn and mixed seeds, and a suet feeder.

LEFT We never saw an American goldfinch in our backyard until my mother added niger seeds to her offerings.

OPPOSITE Bird feeders are available in an ever-increasing array of sizes, shapes and specializations. From left, hanging Droll Yankee big top, wire suet basket on tree, hanging tube feeder, elevated feeding table and hanging mesh bag of suet.

Hanging or pole-mounted feeders are available in a bewildering array of designs and sizes: bowls with baffles over and under them to thwart squirrels and undesirable birds, tubes with trays hanging under them, traditional house and hopper shapes, plastic bins with suction cups for mounting on the outside of your home's windows.

Make the choice based on what appeals to you, but be certain that your feeder is easy to fill, has a large capacity, is easy to take apart for cleaning, has unbreakable plastic for any clear parts, offers protection from the weather and has reinforced openings.

You'll find three types of sunflower seed available from most stores that sell birdseed in bulk: gray-stripe, black-stripe and oil-type. As the Geis study demonstrated, the oil-type is the most preferred, probably because it offers the highest percentage of oil to content and has the thinnest shell.

Birds commonly attracted to hanging or pole-mounted feeders include the American goldfinch, black-capped chickadee, blue jay, Carolina chickadee, common flicker, downy woodpecker, evening grosbeak, hairy woodpecker, house finch, house sparrow, northern cardinal, pine siskin, purple finch, red-breasted nuthatch, scrub jay, starling, tufted titmouse and white-breasted nuthatch. Window feeders generally will attract the tamer species, such as chickadees, nuthatches and titmice.

A niger seed feeder is a hanging tube feeder with very small openings to prevent the tiny seeds from spilling and small perches to allow only certain species – notably the American goldfinch – access to the relatively expensive seeds.

Some authorities, noting results of studies such as that done by Geis and his volunteers, point out that the finches have shown strong preference for the oil-type sunflower seed, and, thus, the separate niger feeder is unnecessary. On the other hand, I remember the joyful hours my mother spent observing the finches that came into our backyard for the first time only after she added a niger feeder. I continue to make the specialized feeder part of my annual offering.

Many backyard birds, like the northern cardinal and the sparrow, prefer to feed on or near the ground. Many species that habitually visit hanging or pole-mounted feeders will also feed at this level.

The simplest ground feeder is a scattering of finely cracked corn and commercial birdseed mix over the ground. A fairly large area, no less than eight feet in diameter, will allow large flocks to feed together and will encourage more natural behavior than the limited, cramped and competitive perching spots available on the hanging feeders. Feeding tables that stand on four legs or a single post a few feet off the ground can also be considered ground feeders in that they will attract the same birds. They should be no less than 3- or 4-feet-square, with a raised edge to keep food within.

ABOVE Small perches such as on this hanging tubular feeder fend off larger birds, saving the relatively expensive niger seeds for intended visitors like the house finch. The larger birds will be content with less-expensive seeds offered at other hanging or ground feeders.

All feeders and baths should offer quick escape routes nearby, such as dense shrubs or a brush pile about eight feet away, but this is even more important for vulnerable, ground-feeding birds. Place the feeders any closer to the cover and it can become a hiding place for the principal land-based threat to the birds – the domestic cat.

The escape cover also provides perches for subordinate birds to await their turns in the flock's pecking order, while the more dominant birds are at the food.

Some of the species attracted to ground feeders are the American crow, black-capped chickadee, blue jay, brown-headed cowbird, common grackle, dark-eyed junco, fox sparrow, house sparrow, mourning dove, northern cardinal, pigeon, red-winged blackbird, rufous-sided towhee, scrub jay, song sparrow, starling, tree sparrow, tufted titmouse, white-crowned sparrow, white-throated sparrow, gamebirds such as the northern bobwhite and ring-necked pheasant.

Suet feeders are filled with the hard fat located around beef kidneys and loins. It provides a source of quick, high energy, a particular favorite of woodpeckers. The welcome treat can be offered in a cage of plastic-coated wire, a nylon mesh bag in which onions were purchased or a small log with a series of one-inch-diameter holes drilled into it. Any of the feeding devices can be attached to a tree or hung from a limb or

another feeder, but squirrels will make short work of any mesh bag that is not out of their reach. Enclosing and securing the suet will prevent large birds from carrying off large chunks, most of which would be lost in flight before they even stopped to eat.

To take suet-feeding one step further, you might want to make your own suet cakes or cones. Cut the suet into small bits, melt it in a pan with a bit of water and mix in your favorite birdseed mixture. If you're making cakes, pour it into muffin tins and let it cool and harden. If you're making suet cones, dip pine cones into the mixture repeatedly until they take on thick globs of the stuff. Let them cool and harden, then attach strings to hang them in various places around the backyard.

Although birds will eat suet year-round, the Cornell University Laboratory of Ornithology recommends that it not be offered when outside temperatures are over 70 degrees Fahrenheit. It can become rancid and harmful to the birds.

Suet feeders will attract a wide array of birds, including the black-capped chickadee, blue jay, Carolina chickadee, downy woodpecker, hairy woodpecker, mockingbird, red-breasted nuthatch, red-headed woodpecker, starling, tufted titmouse and white-breasted nuthatch.

## Special on the menu today

Insect-eaters, such as the nuthatches, will supplement their cold-month diets with the seeds and suet you offer, but you can give them a real treat by offering occasional insect feasts during the dead of winter.

Crickets and mealworms can be purchased from bait and pet shops, and a wide assortment of other insects can be ordered from biological supply houses. But such feeding is prohibitively expensive.

A much more economical means of supplying a buggy feast is to zap it together the previous summer and early fall with one of the electric bug zappers that have come so much into favor in backyards in recent years. On any warm evening, a single zapper will kill and stun hundreds of insects. A bag propped open and hung beneath the zapper will fill quickly with a high-protein snack that can be frozen for later use. If enough supply has been put into the freezer for the coming winter, or if a bug-filled deep freeze is not something that you particularly desire, a tray can be hung beneath the zapper to provide summertime food. Hard-pressed bird parents with nests full of hungry nestlings will welcome the easy supply of nourishing food.

A low-tech method to achieve the same ends creates an artificial, injured tree limb, where insects will quickly congregate and serve up a similar feast for the birds. Paint the limb with a sugar-water solution, similar to that used in

ABOVE Woodpeckers will find themselves sharing the suet feeder, as many other species are drawn to the high-energy food. Here, a red-bellied woodpecker and a starling feed together.

OPPOSITE Suet can be melted and poured into drilled holes in a small log to form a rustic-looking feeder. Here, a tufted titmouse extracts suet from a length of sassafras wood.

particularly welcomed when an extended snow cover keeps the birds from natural supplies. A similar, earthy attraction is a hollow spot on the ground filled with soft loam, in which the birds can take dust baths.

Raisins, currants, other dried or fresh fruit cut into small bits, peanuts in the shell, and eggshells toasted lightly in the oven and crushed have been successful out-of-the-ordinary treats at the feeder. When you try a new food birds may be suspicious at first. If you put it in the feeders they visit regularly, however, they are likely to give it a try.

## Home-grown seed

Another special effort is to grow your own bird seed in your flower garden. Cosmos, four o'clocks, marigolds, petunias, sunflowers and zinnias all lend themselves well to this plan. As late summer and early fall roll around, instead of pulling and discarding fading flowers, let them stand to wither and go to seed. Many birds will attack the feast while it's still in the garden, but you can also gather the seeds, after the flowers have dried, by shaking the flowers over an open bag. The large-head flowers, particularly the sunflowers, can be cut from the stem intact and then saved as a ready-made, midwinter snack table.

## Merry Christmas, everyone

Living Christmas trees, decorated with special treats for wildlife and the animals they attract, have become very popular. The tradition seems to have started as a use for discarded indoor trees. But many backyard birders now look forward to a special Christmas morning out on their lawns as well as in their homes and add an extra bird tree to their Yuletide shopping list.

Popular items, both with the birders and the birds, on the living Christmas tree include strings of peanuts in the shell, popcorn or fresh fruit cut into small bits; whole doughnuts; and net bags filled with dried berries that have been collected the previous summer, including blueberry, dogwood, elderberry, mountain ash and wild cherry. Some particularly festive decorators add old Christmas balls and garland for an extra touch of color on a winter morning.

**ABOVE Mourning doves
quickly become regulars at
ground feeders. Cracked corn
is a favorite food.**

hummingbird feeders, and you've made a natural gathering place for insects. The feeding station may need a fresh coat of solution every day to maintain its potency and efficiency.

Wintering insect-eaters are also quick to take advantage of nontypical, yet high-protein foods, such as cheese, bacon, diced raw meat and crumbled dry dog food. Peanut butter is another high-energy food, which also provides needed salt. Mix it with equal amounts of corn meal to prevent caking and clogging in the birds' mouths and throats, and spread it on tree limbs and trunks.

Grit – the tiny, rough particles that birds ingest to help with their digestion – also can be a bonus feeder. Sand particles and crushed seashells can be bought for this purpose in pet shops, bird supply stores and feed stores. Offered in a shallow pan, it will be used throughout the year but

**OPPOSITE Extend those warm
Yuletide feelings to the birds
with a living Christmas tree
decorated with food items.
Throw in a few old Christmas
balls and you can create a
truly festive scene.**

## Hummers: A special case

You won't find hummingbirds at any of the above feeders. Not only because they spend the winter months far south of the U.S.-Mexican border, but also because none of this food appeals to them.

A yard filled with flowers is the best attraction, and we'll discuss that later. Tubular feeder bottles filled with a sugar-water solution is the artificial answer. Solutions ranging from two parts water to one part sugar to nine parts water to one part sugar have been recommended. The Cornell laboratory suggests nothing less than four parts water to one part sugar. Whatever solution you settle upon, boil it for two minutes and it will be ready for the hummers.

Many recipes also specify the use of red dye. Apart from the chemical this introduces into the bird's system, it is unnecessary. True, red is the number one attractive color for hummingbirds; experimentation has proven that. But a red bow or plastic flower will be just as effective in getting the birds to your feeder.

The feeder can be anything from commercially available designs to hamster bottles to test tubes with rubber stoppers. The most crucial element is ease of cleaning. Every hummingbird feeder should be cleaned no less than every other day. Dangerous mold may grow in solution that ferments in the sun, leading to a disease that attacks the bird's tongue and eventually kills the bird.

## The right location

Whether it's an elaborate living Christmas tree or just a handful of cracked corn tossed on the ground, the overriding reason for feeding the birds is to bring them closer for intimate observations. Situating your feeder just a few feet from the living room window might at first seem the best location.

However, if you are just starting a feeding program or trying to attract some of the shier birds, such an arrangement might lead to disappointment. The birds might wait weeks before taking advantage of your offerings. Instead, first place your feeder near trees and shrubs the birds are already frequenting. Gradually, move the feeder closer to the desired final location a couple feet a day. Move it just before you fill it at night. Their morning hunger will help the birds to overlook the fact that the feeder is not exactly where they remember it.

In planning each location, try to place your feeders where they are protected from cold winter winds, such as on the downwind side of buildings or natural windbreaks like evergreen trees and shrubs.

ABOVE Feeders can draw many birds quite close for careful observation and detailed photography. If you're new to feeding, you may have to start with the feeders a bit farther from the window and gradually move them closer.

OPPOSITE Research that shows red to be the most attractive color to hummingbirds has led to a proliferation of commercially produced, red feeders.

Also, keep in mind the possibilities of birds crashing into your windows, especially when frightened. They might see reflections of open space in the glass and think they have a clear flight path. Hawk silhouettes, mobiles and the like have cleared up this problem at many backyard feeders.

Keep each location, and every feeder, as clean as possible. Any seeds that aren't eaten within a few days and the hulls from those that are should be removed regularly, even from ground feeders. In addition, areas beneath elevated feeders and the ground feeder locations themselves should be raked periodically.

A periodic scrubbing with a bottle brush, water and a mild detergent is in order for any feeder. Several feeder diseases, including aflatoxin, asperfillus fumigatus, histoplasmosis and salmonellosis, can spread quickly among birds using a dirty feeder, weakening and killing them. All are caused by fungus or bacteria growing in moldy seed, transmitted through the birds' droppings.

## What's an "undesirable"?

Many books, under a heading of troubleshooting and "undesirables," discuss means of thwarting some bird species and all squirrels in their efforts to eat at feeders. Methods for defending against hawks and domestic cats in their efforts to eat smaller birds at the feeders also are offered. I don't acknowledge a label of "undesirable" on any wild creature.

Cowbirds, grackles, pigeons, sparrows, starlings and squirrels are natural parts of the habitat you've created. All can offer their own glimpses into natural history, just as much as a tufted titmouse or a flock of grosbeaks. They can be encouraged to eat cheap seed, table scraps and old bread at ground feeders, while leaving the more expensive sunflower and niger seeds to other species. Simply offering the ground feeder generally is enough for the birds.

Squirrels may need the added discouragement of feeders moved beyond their jumping distance from nearby trees and shrubs – 12 feet is usually enough – and equipped with baffles around poles and wires leading to them.

Likewise, hawks are a natural part of the environment. They just happen to be higher on the food chain than the songbirds, making the birds at the feeder their natural prey. Like all birds of prey, the sharp-shinned and Cooper's hawks – the most regular predators on feeder birds – are protected under federal law. If you want to give the prey a bit of an edge, provide plenty of escape and hiding cover in the form of dense shrubs and brush piles 8 to 10 feet from your feeders.

That same distance works against domestic cats, which are unnatural but skillful killers on the backyard scene. By placing shrubs and brush piles that far from feeders, they become escape routes for the birds rather than hiding places for cats. Birds will also quickly learn to identify a bell around a cat's neck as a signal of impending danger. In addition, cat-proof fences are available commercially.

.....................

**LEFT** Hawks, such as this American kestrel, will take an occasional small songbird, although their reputation for this is greatly exaggerated. When you witness an attack, remember that death is a natural part of life in the wild.

.....................

.....................

**OPPOSITE** Some backyard birders put a great deal of effort into thwarting squirrels. Another approach (INSET) offers the squirrels relatively inexpensive food, such as cracked corn, at ground feeders to draw their attention from hanging feeders filled with more costly items. The squirrels seem content with this arrangement and can provide their own brand of entertaining observation.

.....................

# 2

## Water, a key element

OPPOSITE Birds often seem to
lose all caution when the
opportunity for a good soaking
bath presents itself.

29

Water often seems to come into the backyard as an afterthought on our part. An ornate birdbath would add just the right touch to that spot by the fence. A small pond would really set off that area between the feeding stations. A trickling waterfall would bring life to that rock wall.

But birds take that same water more seriously. To them, it is as basic and universal a daily need as food and protection from their enemies. Food preferences vary widely, but all birds drink water. Many insist on their regular baths as well. Observe the relish with which a song sparrow or a flock of freshly dusted starlings attacks a birdbath and you'll wonder that they would even visit a yard that did not offer water.

For bathing and drinking, water is a tremendous bird attractor. They need it year-round to survive, and they'll gather in greater numbers and greater variety in a habitat that includes it along with food and shelter.

## Water in many forms

Birds are not very fussy about how their water is provided. Rain puddles are just fine, when they're available. They satisfy the few demands that their avian bathers do make. Even rain or dew on plants will do in a pinch.

So, the choice is yours, ranging from a simple pan of water set out daily in the same location to a full-size pond capable of floating a flock of mallards. In general, birds will be content with whatever your yard size, financial constraints and personal inclinations will allow. Of course, the more extensive the arrangement, the more bird needs it will serve, but not without additional space, effort and expense.

A pan, overturned garbage-can lid or pedestal birdbath can be placed almost anywhere. Even a window box at a yardless apartment can hold a pan of water. It will require daily, or more frequent, refills and regular cleaning. Cost will be quite low.

A patio or small yard, at the least, is needed for an in-ground mini-pond with a pipe or hose system for a constant supply of fresh water. Prefabricated fiberglass, cement and ceramic mini-ponds of varying dimensions are available from most garden supply shops.

A do-it-yourself approach is simply to dig a hole and line it with a layer of cushioning sand covered with a tough, plastic liner or with a layer of poured cement. Such ponds can support limited aquatic life, including plants, frogs and fish, in addition to providing a larger birdbath. But, being larger, the mini-pond also will be more of a cleaning chore and will cost more than the pan of water or pedestal birdbath.

A full-scale pond is beyond the capabilities of the average backyard of less than a half-acre. It probably will have its own natural supply of water and won't need refilling attention, but it also can come with a natural supply of potential problems: local ordinances, neighbors' complaints and liability insurance, to name a few. The cost of such a project can reach into the thousands.

ABOVE Water sources can be
as simple as this jar hung from
a tree limb which attracted a
female Scott's oriole.

OPPOSITE Fledglings, like
this young cardinal, often are
reluctant to take their first
baths. But, once they become
acquainted with the water,
they delight in a splash.

31

Most birders will offer something closer to the pan of water than the pond, but, regardless of size and intricacy, all water intended for use by birds must offer certain qualities.

## A few criteria

Birds prefer to bathe knee-deep and to gradually wade into that depth from shallower water. Two-and-a-half to three inches is their maximum, and the bottom should slope gradually from a half-inch at the edge to that "deep" section in the center. A larger pond, with much greater center depths, must provide an expanse of edge that does not drop beyond the three-inch maximum.

The feathered bathers prefer a rough bottom that gives them sure footing as they wade into the water. Cement surfaces feel secure underfoot. Some plastic and ceramic birdbaths do not, but a layer of small pebbles and sand will make the birds feel at home in them as well.

Birds also need a sense of security around the bath. A wet bird has a more difficult time in taking flight and is vulnerable to waiting predators, such as neighborhood cats, that might be lurking nearby. Pedestal and hanging birdbaths remove most of this threat, because while cats might be able to leap to their raised levels, they probably won't be able to snatch a bird at the same time. But these off-the-ground sources rob earth-bound animals of the water.

An in-ground or on-the-ground water supply can be made safer by removing all brush and shrubbery from a 3½ to 4-foot area around the water. With the brush and shrubbery go the potential hiding places for predators. The open area can be left grassy, planted with moist-area plants that will not grow large enough to provide new hiding places, or covered with fine sand to add a dusting area to the habitat.

An overhanging branch – the thornier the better – that will not support the weight of a cat offers bathing birds a quick escape route and a spot for fluffing, drying and preening after the bath. Similar perches in shrubs and trees about 10 feet from the water's edge also will be welcome. A third perch can be made from a sturdy tree limb, held in place in the center of the water source by a sand-filled, submerged coffee can. All of these same arrangements also will offer lookout perches for approaching birds to scan the area before dropping to the water.

**OPPOSITE Birds prefer shallow water no deeper than 2½ to 3 inches. This is a Brewer's blackbird.**

**ABOVE A common grackle quenches its thirst while perched on the rim of a plastic, pedestal-type bird bath.**

## Some special problems

Birdbath water must be kept clean or it will become a breeding ground for disease quite quickly. In larger ponds, with natural aquatic life and constant sources of fresh water, recirculating and cleansing generally will be a self-sustaining cycle. But smaller supplies that are not recirculated and replenished automatically will need daily changes. In addition, the birdbath surface should be cleaned weekly with a stiff brush.

In winter months across much of North America, there is a constant struggle to keep the water from freezing. Emptying the birdbath and tipping it onto its side until spring is the unfortunate alternative chosen by many birders. They're taking the artificial source away at the same time that droughtlike conditions – frozen and inaccessible natural sources – confront the wildlife.

With just a bit more effort or expense, they could help to ease the strain and, at the same time, greatly enhance the drawing power of their winter feeding program. A pan of fresh, warm – not hot – water will offer a few hours of drinking and bathing before freezing. An aquarium heater or submersible birdbath heater will keep birdbaths and mini-ponds open, as will a light bulb in the base of a pedestal bath.

## The special appeal of moving water

Any time of the year, whatever aquatic arrangements the birder provides can be made even more attractive with the sound of falling or running water. It's an irresistible magnet for many species. A dripping hose hanging over the birdbath or a suspended bucket, dripping through a small nail hole in its side about a half-inch above its bottom, will supply the motion simply and cheaply. A spray or mist-fountain can be placed in the center of a mini-pond or large birdbath. A mini-pond can be built as a series of tiered pools, one emptying into another. In addition to drawing birds and other wildlife, the moving water will add a very real sense of the natural world to the backyard.

**PREVIOUS PAGE This pair of yellow-billed magpies seems to be waiting to share a drink with the next passerby.**

**ABOVE A wood thrush, attracted by the sound of moving water, wades for a drink in a small backyard pond.**

ABOVE Water in bird baths
should be changed daily, as
drinking and bathing visitors
tend to foul fresh water
quickly. This is a male house
finch.

# 3

## Planting for birds

OPPOSITE This tree provides a
rich source of insects for this
mountain bluebird to feed to
its nestlings.

39

A<small>N ACQUAINTANCE</small> moved to the suburbs for amenities such as open space and fresh air. Her new house sits on a bit of space, about a half-acre, of which she is quite proud. It's a nice neighborhood. Many of the backyards have been planted in an array of flowers, ground covers, shrubs and trees, offering a haven for man and bird alike.

Her property, however, is a sterile square of barren lawn and a few struggling ornamentals, much of which turns brown at the slightest hint of a dry spell. The lawn has been drenched with pesticides and herbicides. Nothing lives there, and it's not the kind of place where you want to walk barefoot through the grass.

My acquaintance curses her neighbors for attracting birds and other wildlife into the neighborhood. She hates their feeding efforts and ponders why they would perpetuate plants that bring these intruders near, and sometimes onto, her 21,780 square feet. The world would be a better place without the myriad of problems that these creatures bring with them, she claims.

In my book, the world would be a better place if she had moved to an apartment in the city and left that half-acre for someone who saw it as more than a flat surface for giving parties. In this day of vanishing habitat, a suburban backyard, any backyard anywhere, is much too valuable a commodity to waste on single-minded use that doesn't include wildlife.

Fortunately, a growing number of property owners agree. They understand that a healthy backyard with a thriving population of wild creatures is also a healthy place for people. In the United States alone, there are an estimated 12 million of them.

....................
**RIGHT Diversity is crucial in a backyard designed to attract birds. Here, a mockingbird feeds on sumac.**
....................

## Natural doesn't mean messy

A natural-looking backyard, filled with everything from lawn to tree, is not necessarily an unkempt backyard. On the contrary, it often implies a careful selection of plants for purposes far beyond mere ornamentation. Planning and implementing a backyard habitat with wildlife in mind is an involved and meticulous process.

Each plant placed there serves a purpose, or several purposes among three of the four basic needs for survival:

● Food, such as berries, seeds and fruits: It is prolific? Does the combination of different species provide a continuous menu throughout the seasons? Do some of them hold their fruits into or through the winter?

● Protective cover: Does it offer escape and protection for enemies? Does it offer winter protection from the elements?

● Safe nesting: Are the nesting spots inaccessible to predators?

Diversity is crucial in a backyard designed to attract birds and other wildlife. Different needs are served at each level of plant life: grass and ground cover, up to 1 foot; shrubs, 1 to 5 feet; small trees, 5 to 15 feet; and tall trees, more than 15 feet.

**ABOVE Barberry berries
provide food throughout the
long winter months.**

The American robin, for example, is attracted to a mix of open lawn for hunting worms, shrubs, small trees and a few mature trees for protective cover and safe nesting. Woodpeckers prefer backyards with large, mature trees, where they can find their diet of tree-dwelling insects. The yellow-bellied sapsucker favors ash and elderberry for their saps. Warblers, vireos, chickadees and flycatchers are attracted to willows for their excellent insect-attracting ability. Ground and shrub nesters, such as a rufous-sided towhee, need thickets 3 to 10 feet tall and at least 6 feet wide.

If you're starting from a bare, manicured lawn, shrubs will show the quickest results. Trees can take years of special care before they even approach their full potential as bird habitat. Shrubs can be of benefit almost immediately, particularly when planted as hedges or clusters throughout the property. They can make your backyard home to a myriad of birds while you wait for your trees to mature.

## Let nature give you a hand

You won't even need to visit a nursery for some shrubs, as well as vines and grasses, if you're willing to allow the birds to decide what you plant through a method known as perch planting. In late summer or early fall, prepare a 5-foot-wide strip as you would if you were going to plant vegetables. Make it the length that you want your hedgerow. Into the strip set a staggered line of fence posts, 15 to 20 feet apart. Stretch heavy wire or cord between the posts, one strand 5 feet and another 1 foot above the ground. Birds will perch on these strands, and any seeds in their droppings will be planted into your future hedgerow. Once you have established it, don't be afraid to work it as you would a hedgerow of stock bought at the nursery. Both the plants and the birds will benefit from a severe trimming in the fall. The shrubs will respond with thicker, healthier growth and added nooks and angles for nesting birds.

This perch-planting method can grow into quite a wild spot, and some of the plants the birds contribute might offend neighbors who aren't as wildlife-minded as you, so arrange this in a secluded part of the backyard.

The same caution applies to another natural planting method, the wild food patch, which is designed to supply seed-eaters such as the American goldfinch and redpoll. Plan

the patch as five strips of equal width, each no less than five feet wide. In sequence over the next five years, plow one strip under each year. The plowing will halt any significant shrub growth, while encouraging a rich blend of weeds. Panic grasses, ragweed and lambsquarter are among the species to expect the first year. Aster, goldenrod and milkweed will appear by the third. You can supplement the volunteer growth with plantings of mixed corn, grain, sorghum, millet and sunflower.

## Some excellent choices

New backyard habitat planners often worry that their choices in plants won't match the choices of the birds they are trying to attract. It's generally a needless concern. Selecting plants that birds won't find some use for may be more difficult than finding those that will attract them. So varied is the plant preference range of our feathered visitors.

For example, raspberry and blackberry are known to provide food in one form or another to more than 145 bird species; elder, 120; dogwood, grape and blueberry, more than 90; bayberry and cherry, 85; oak and pine, more than 60; red cedar, 55; and spruce, 30.

Nurserymen generally are familiar with not only the plants they sell but also how those plants fit into the local environment, including their usefulness to wildlife. They are also your best source in learning which plants from the following list of those that attract many species of birds are best suited for your region:

Ground covers and vines: bearberry, catbrier, cloudberry, dewberry, crowberry, grape, greenbrier, ground juniper, honeysuckle, pokeberry, rose, sarsaparilla, serviceberry, strawberry, Virginia creeper, wintergreen, yaupon.

Shrubs, deciduous: barberry, bayberry, beloperone, blackberry, blueberry, buffaloberry, butterfly bush, currant, dogwood, elderberry, firethorn, hawthorn, holly, honeysuckle, osoberry, privet, serviceberry, sumac, trumpet creeper, viburnum, Virginia creeper.

Shrubs, evergreen: buckthorn, cotoneaster, holly, huckleberry, inkberry, juniper, rhododendron, salal, yew.

Trees, deciduous: alder, ash, aspen, beech, birch, blackgum, black cherry, choke cherry, crabapple, dogwood, hackberry, hickory, maple, mountain ash, mulberry, oak, pecan, persimmon, Russian olive.

Trees, evergreen: Douglas fir, hemlock, holly, ironwood, juniper, larch, madrone, pine, red cedar, spruce.

These lists are not intended to be exclusive of other plant species. They offer some of the common species that will grow in a wide range of habitats and attract several species of birds. Many other plants are equally beneficial in the backyard habitat.

**OPPOSITE Blue jays seek out large food items, such as the seeds on this sunflower pod. Acorns are another favorite that a backyard habitat can provide.**

ABOVE & OPPOSITE Every
plant in a fully developed
backyard wildlife habitat
serves a purpose: a thorny
barberry hedge is home to a
mockingbird's nest (ABOVE),
and a tree provides a safe
nesting place for these two
young mourning doves
(OPPOSITE).

ABOVE & OPPOSITE Different birds have different needs in protective nesting cover, from the wood thrush's nest in the crook of a tree (ABOVE), to the red-shafted flicker's nest in a tree cavity (OPPOSITE).

## Some special concerns

Once again, hummingbirds are a special concern. Their interest in plants is confined to the flower, the nectar it produces and sometimes the insects that gather at it. Experiments have determined (see Chapter 1 on feeding and feeders) that red, followed by yellow, is their number one choice in flowers.

Some plants with flowers known to attract hummingbirds are azalea, bee balm, bellflower, blue bell, bouncing betty, butterfly bush, canna, cardinal flower, century plant, columbine, coral bells, cornflower, day lily, delphinium, erythriana, figwort, flowering tobacco, four o'clock, foxglove, fuchsia, gladiolus, hamelia, hollyhock, iris, jasmine, jewelweed.

Larkspur, lilac, lily, lousewort, matrimony vine, milkweed, mint, monkey flower, morning glory, nasturtium, painted cup, pelargonium, penstemon, petunia, phlox, poinciana, poppy, ragged robin, rattlesnake root, scabious, scarlet sage, snapdragon, Solomon's seal, spiderflower, sweet william, torch lily and trumpet creeper.

Some of these, such as columbine and coral bells, will produce springtime flowers. Others, such as cardinal flower and delphinium, will give summertime flowers. A blend, combined with manmade hummingbird feeders, should keep the tiny birds in the backyard over a longer period of time than any one species could.

Likewise, for many other bird species, your selection of plants should include some that carry their fruits and berries into the winter as a source of bird food. Some of these are barberry, bayberry, bush honeysuckle, cotoneaster, crabapple, cranberry bush, hackberry, hawthorn, holly, juniper, mountain ash, red cedar, Russian olive, sumac and Virginia creeper.

## Don't forget whose backyard it is

Backyard wildlife habitats need not be impenetrable jungles or uninviting quagmires. Open lawn areas bordered by thickets, with the wildlife they attract, add their own charm to lawn parties. A pathway of flat stones leading to a bench beneath an ivy-covered arbor offers a tranquil setting for a brief respite.

Don't restrict your garden planning; not every inch, nor every plant, must be decided solely with wildlife in mind. If a vegetable garden is part of your ideal backyard, have a vegetable garden. If an ornamental shrub appeals to you, but offers no apparent wildlife value, plant it for its ornamentation. The wildlife will make do with the rest of the yard that you have designed for them.

....................
**TOP & ABOVE** Even plants intended for strictly ornamental purposes can provide for birds, as a pair of chipping sparrows prove with their nest in the tall evergreen shrub on the far right.
....................

....................
**LEFT** Flowers are the key to tempting hummingbirds into your backyard. Red is the most attractive color.
....................

# 4

# Nestboxes and other help

OPPOSITE Blue jays have
earned a reputation as nest
robbers, a reputation that is
justified but exaggerated.

As a growing and thriving North America entered the 1900s, migrating flocks of 200 or more bluebirds were common sights each March and October. Gardens everywhere supported breeding pairs of the birds each summer.

By 1963, annual bird counts had registered the lowest bluebird numbers on record. Some estimates placed the total population at just 10 per cent of what it once was. Sightings of the colorful little bird were something at which to marvel.

Since the late 1970s, annual counts such as the Breeding Bird Survey Program of the U.S. Fish and Wildlife Service have shown the population to be on the increase, particularly in the past three years.

The 20th century has been a roller coaster ride of an existence for the bluebird, and man has had a major role in both the downs and the ups. As the continent was developed, huge chunks of the bird's habitat were destroyed. Hedgerows and the accompanying nesting snags were removed for more efficient farming techniques and to make way for housing and commercial developments. Orchard growers switched to smaller tree stock, constantly pruning away any deadwood that might provide nesting cavities. Pasture fence posts, once offering miles of rotting, cavity-filled wooden posts, became the domain of solid metal posts.

Man also brought to the continent two new competitors for the dwindling nesting spots. The bluebird, which had successfully competed with all native fauna, suddenly faced the extra challenge of the immigrant house sparrow and starling. The house sparrow not only usurps the bluebird's nesting cavities, but attacks and evicts the bluebird at every stage of nesting, sometimes killing adult and nestling alike.

Nature entered the fray in 1957 with a harsh winter that claimed an estimated one-third to one-half of the migrant flocks in the South. In an unrelentless attack, a half-dozen hard winters followed, and what was left of the bluebird population crashed.

**ABOVE The house sparrow, a species that was introduced to North America in the 1850s, is one of two chief competitors for the native bluebird's nesting cavities. The other is the starling.**

**OPPOSITE Nestboxes have played a significant role in the reversal of declining bluebird populations.**

But, when the bluebird had reached its lowest point and was teetering on the edge, man stepped in again. Individuals, regional groups and, by 1978, the North American Bluebird Society gave the bird what it needed most for a comeback – cavity nesting sites. The natural snags and fence posts were largely gone, but manmade boxes – entire trails of them – sprang up. And with the growing supply of nesting sites, the bluebird's decline began to reverse.

The bluebird can still use a lot of help, so it's a prime candidate if you want to offer nestboxes. However, it does like open spaces. The nestbox should be 100 feet from dense shrubbery or thickets, which makes it an impractical choice for many small backyards. One of the other more than 50 species that have been observed nesting in manmade boxes – 30 are regular tenants – might have more affinity for the habitat you've created. Maybe a two-sided nesting platform and a plateful of mud will lure a pair of robins to set up housekeeping. A couple house wrens might take over a tiny box hung from a limb.

For some species properly constructed nestboxes are the most effective attractant. House wrens, for example, are almost exclusively insect-eaters. Feeders generally won't bring them in. But a small box, with an entrance hole of exactly 1¼ inches, hung from a tree limb is like a magnet. The small hole excludes the wren's stiffest nesting competitors – house sparrows and starlings – and protects the nest area from predators. The swinging of a hanging, rather than stationary pole-mounted, box has the same effect.

## Maybe something in a different style?

Each species – and often individual birds – has its own likes and dislikes in a nestbox. A box that meets the exact specifications is more likely to attract an intended species, but any box that comes close will attract some bird attention. Likewise, if you don't like the tenant you attract in one location, move the box to a different type of habitat after the first group of fledglings has departed. As with all elements of backyard birding, the more variety you offer, the more species you will attract.

Nuthatches, woodpeckers and tufted titmice prefer their nestboxes to be made of hollowed logs or boards with the bark still on them. A prime location is under or on a limb of the largest tree in the yard.

The purple martin house is the most instantly identifiable nestbox. Few birds are willing to nest within such close proximity, particularly with others of their own kind. The bluebird insists on at least 100 yards between nestboxes. The robin has been known to nest within 25 feet of others of its own kind. But the martin eagerly settles into 10- to 30-room, close-quartered apartment complexes, if it arrives from

LEFT One of the most familiar nestboxes is the purple martin house. Here, a successful colony features abundant housing, open spaces and access to a pond or lake. Many pairs of purple martins will share the same house (INSET), each pair in its own apartment. Houses of as many as 200 apartments have been constructed. The average is 10 to 30.

migration before starlings and house sparrows have occupied the box. To help the intended tenant take ownership, don't put up the house until the first martins arrive on the scene in the spring. If you're lucky enough to attract a few pairs, chances are they'll return with additional tenants next year.

ABOVE To some species, like this eastern phoebe, a nestbox is not a box at all, but simply a shelf on the side of a building.

Phoebes won't bring other pairs back the next year, but they will return to nest in the same eaves of your home or outbuilding, which is their one requirement. House finches are even less fussy. Their nests have been found in everything from eaves to old tin cans.

House sparrows stick close to man, nesting in eaves, rafters, drainpipes, ivy on walls, natural cavities and nestboxes. Barn owls, on the other hand, prefer nestboxes in secluded spots or seldom-used outbuildings.

Screech owls, which can be valuable allies of anyone with a mouse problem, won't nest lower than 10 feet above the ground. Song sparrows opt for nesting on the ground, in low bushes or on open nest-shelves placed no more than 3 feet off the ground.

In addition to such locational preferences, birds have their individual size preferences. The diameter of the entrance is the most important of these for many species because it can deter larger birds from usurping the nestbox from its intended occupants and protect the contents from predators.

---

The U.S. Fish and Wildlife Service recommends the following nestbox dimensions for some common species:

**Species**

| FLOOR (SQ. IN.) | DEPTH (IN.) | ENTRANCE ABOVE FLOOR (IN.) | ENTRANCE DIAMETER (IN.) | ABOVE GROUND (FT.) |
|---|---|---|---|---|
| **American Kestrel** | | | | |
| 11 × 11 | 12 | 9 to 12 | 3 × 4 | 20 to 30 |
| **American robin** | | | | |
| 6 × 8 | 8 | sides open | | 6 to 15 |
| **Barn owl** | | | | |
| 10 × 18 | 15 to 18 | 4 | 6 | 12 to 18 |
| **Barn swallow** | | | | |
| 6 × 6 | 6 | sides open | | 8 to 12 |
| **Black-capped chickadee** | | | | |
| 4 × 4 | 8 to 10 | 6 to 8 | 1⅛ | 6 to 15 |
| **Carolina wren** | | | | |
| 4 × 4 | 6 to 8 | 1 to 6 | 1½ | 6 to 10 |
| **Common flicker** | | | | |
| 7 × 7 | 16 to 18 | 14 to 16 | 2½ | 6 to 20 |
| **Downy woodpecker** | | | | |
| 4 × 4 | 9 to 12 | 6 to 8 | 1¼ | 6 to 20 |
| **Eastern bluebird** | | | | |
| 5 × 5 | 8 | 6 | 1½ | 5 |
| **European starling** | | | | |
| 6 × 6 | 16 to 18 | 14 to 16 | 2 | 10 to 25 |
| **Hairy woodpecker** | | | | |
| 6 × 6 | 12 to 15 | 9 to 12 | 1½ | 12 to 20 |
| **House wren** | | | | |
| 4 × 4 | 8 to 10 | 1 to 6 | 1 to 1¼ | 6 to 10 |
| **Screech owl** | | | | |
| 8 × 8 | 12 to 15 | 9 to 12 | 3 | 10 to 30 |
| **Tree swallow** | | | | |
| 5 × 5 | 6 to 8 | 5 to 6 | 1½ | 6 to 16 |
| **Tufted titmouse** | | | | |
| 4 × 4 | 8 to 10 | 6 to 8 | 1¼ | 6 to 15 |
| **White-breasted nuthatch** | | | | |
| 4 × 4 | 8 to 10 | 6 to 8 | 1¼ | 12 to 20 |
| **Wood duck** | | | | |
| 10 × 18 | 10 to 24 | 12 to 16 | 4 | 10 to 20 |

Despite their many differences, nestboxes have some criteria they all should share. Wood is the best material. It will remain cooler in summer and warmer in winter than materials such as metal or pottery. Pine, red cedar and cypress all hold up well to the rigors of outdoor use. Boxes held together by screws will be sturdier and longer-lasting than those constructed with nails. A roof overhang of two to three inches will shelter the entrance hole and interior from even driving rains.

. . . . . . . . . . . . . . . . . . . .

**ABOVE Nestboxes can be made from many materials, although wood will be cooler in the summer and warmer in the winter than most other common materials.**

. . . . . . . . . . . . . . . . . . . .

. . . . . . . . . . . . . . . . . . . .

**LEFT With adaptations for different sizes, this basic bluebird nestbox can house many different species.**

. . . . . . . . . . . . . . . . . . . .

Cavity-nesting birds have no need for perches on the outside of their nestboxes. They can easily cling to the wood's surface, but the usurping house sparrow has a tough time occupying a box without a perch.

Birds may be suspicious of a nestbox placed on the main trunk of a tree because of past experiences with climbing predators. Mounting the box on a nearby post may allay their fears, while encircling the post with a sheath of metal or a climbing baffle will actually solve the predator problem.

A similar wariness of new boxes can be eliminated by positioning them the previous October or November to weather through the winter. Some birds might use them as roosting shelters on cold nights and, when the nesting season rolls around, no new disturbing elements need be added.

As with feeders, you will want to clean nestboxes regularly to prevent the spread of disease and parasites. Since some birds bring off more than one brood during the season, take care of this chore just as soon as the first set of fledglings has left the nest and you may attract a second tenant. A hinged roof or a sliding side panel will make the job much easier.

## A bit of string, a strand of hair

You can encourage even those birds with no interest in your nestboxes to nest in your backyard, or at least nearby, by offering a ready supply of nesting materials. Chipping and song sparrows are quick to take advantage of human or animal hair. Swallows appreciate small feathers. Orioles will grab bits of knitting yarn for their distinctive, hanging basket nests. Wrens like an ample supply of small twigs.

Materials such as string and yarn can be draped over a washline cord, tree or shrub branch, fence, whatever is handy. Each strand should be no longer than six to eight inches. Any longer and it could loop and strangle or tangle the bird. String, yarn and cotton thread can also be hung in mesh onion bags with other materials such as feathers, straw and hair. Additional bags can be staked to the ground and hung from low shrub branches, providing materials to potential nesters at every level.

Eggshells, lightly toasted in the oven and crushed, are another welcome, special offering during the nesting season. Birds such as the American goldfinch, barn swallow, bluebirds, blue jay, flickers, house sparrow, kingbirds, orioles and tree sparrow make short work of the rich source of calcium carbonate. Some observers claim that the availability of eggshells also decreases nest-robbing by blue jays.

BELOW When building their nests, many species of birds accept handouts like the bits of yarn that will line this mockingbird's nest.

ABOVE Shredded strips from a discarded, plastic bread bag are being incorporated into this common grackle's nest-in-progress.

OPPOSITE Sometimes birds can use a hand from man: this chipping sparrow's nest was saved from a fall.

## "Unwanted" tenants

A well-protected, snug cavity is a much-sought-after commodity to many wild creatures, feathered and furred alike. They generally see no great differences between those provided by nature and those provided by man, and man's intended tenant isn't even a passing thought. As a result, starlings are perfectly content to nest in the box to which you had hoped to attract wrens, despite the possible tight fit. Likewise, house sparrows will jump at a cozy little bluebird box. Both problems have solutions that can be applied to many other species.

The larger starling needs an entrance hole of no less than two inches in diameter, while the largest hole that any wren could need is 1¼ inches. Drill the correct size hole, and the starlings will look elsewhere. Follow the size specifications listed above to offer nestboxes to other species that you want to attract and to exclude those that you don't.

Bluebirds prefer boxes somewhat removed from human dwellings and mounted no more than five feet above the ground. Their competitors, the house sparrows, prefer to remain quite close to man, and they look for nesting sites higher than five feet.

Squirrels, too, are attracted to the potential new home sites, however they generally need to enlarge the holes to gain entry. A strip of sheet metal attached over the edges of the holes will prevent them from gnawing their way into the boxes. The metal should have no projecting, sharp edges that could injure nesting birds.

## That "orphan" probably isn't

Another situation that you will run into if you attract birds to nest in your backyard is the "orphaned" baby bird. The vision that comes immediately to mind is that of a speckle-breasted baby robin in a shoe box filled with grass and a young boy asking, "Can I keep it? Its mother left it." Well, she probably did not abandon the baby. Even if the parents are not apparent when you come across the young bird, they are more than likely close at hand. Give them some time to return to what they were doing, possibly before you interrupted them. Carefully place the baby bird in a protected spot, such as a shrub, return inside and watch from a window. Chances favor the momentary return of a parent bird. Perhaps it has been off tending to the siblings of the one you located.

**OPPOSITE This fledgling blue jay may appear alone in the world, but is actually waiting for a delivery of food from its parents.**

**ABOVE Backyard nestboxes open new aspects of the birds' lives to you, such as this house wren cleaning the box by removing the fecal sacs of its nestlings.**

LEFT With nests of hungry
young to keep supplied with
high-protein food, parent
birds will remove an
enormous amount of harmful
insects from the backyard.
These are tree swallows.

On the other hand, if you know that no parent will be coming, for example, because the neighbor's cats killed the adult robins, it's time to take action. Be aware that you're undertaking an immense task that has every chance of a heartbreaking failure. Birds feed their young every few minutes all day. If the baby bird hasn't yet opened its eyes, the lowest frequency that it will be able to get by on is at least every half-hour. If the eyes are opened and flight feathers have begun to emerge, the feeding schedule can be lessened to hourly intervals.

The baby bird will need plenty of protein. Small pieces of the very best canned dog food, dipped in raw egg yolk, have proven successful. Everything must be room temperature. Place it into the back of the baby bird's mouth. As the chick matures, it can be given worms and other soft insects. When it wants to peck at the insects itself, allow it to do so.

The chick must be kept in a warm enclosure, lined with soft material. For those still in down, 95 degrees Fahrenheit is needed, decreasing gradually to 70 degrees by the time they are fledged. A 60-watt light bulb nearby will turn the trick. It can be moved to adjust the temperature inside the "nest".

## A box for winter

On particularly cold winter nights, birds may seek out nestboxes that haven't been taken in for the season as protected roosting shelters. However, a few slight twists on the summertime nestbox design will result in an even more attractive and useful winter roosting shelter.

First, begin thinking in terms of larger scale. For even the smallest birds a roosting shelter should have a 10-square-inch base and be 3 feet from base to ceiling. Several birds will often roost together, sharing the collective body heat. The entrance hole should be just 2 inches above the base so the entire shelter can act as a trap for the rising heat generated by the occupants. Quarter-inch dowel rods, glued into holes on the inside walls of the shelter and staggered so that the birds won't be roosting directly above one another, will encourage more birds to use the box. Place it on a pole or tree, 10 feet off the ground, in a sheltered spot with the entrance hole facing south, away from the winter winds.

Squirrels will be attracted to the shelter as a potential den site, and predators will be attracted for the potential meal inside. But the same measures used to thwart them at nestboxes in summer or feeders any time of the year will do the job at the winter roosting shelter.

**RIGHT Occasionally a baby bird will become orphaned, and human care is its last hope for survival.**

# 5

## Planning your new habitat

OPPOSITE Is there anything
quite so "ahhhhh-inspiring"
as a tuft-headed robin chick?

67

I F YOU do nothing whatsoever with your backyard, nature will eventually give you a backyard habitat. Unfortunately, some of nature's choices will also give you plenty of headaches with your neighbors, and quite possibly local zoning laws.

A more proactive approach will not only avoid some of these conflicts, but can be an enjoyable learning experience as well with a strong sense of accomplishment awaiting its conclusion. Plans falling short of their desired outcomes can teach as much, or more, than those giving the exact predetermined results. You'll experience both in establishing a backyard habitat for birds.

## A starting point

Your first step is to decide how far you want to go to attract birds. A winter feeding program can be as simple as a feeder and some birdseed. A year-round total habitat, constantly alive with movement and song, may come only after years of painstaking effort and a great deal of expense.

Only you can decide; and even after you do, nothing is written in stone. A half-finished thicket is half-a-thicket more than bare lawn. Some birds will use the part that's finished. And, given time, nature may very likely complete the project.

With your starting goals in mind, consider which of the four basic needs for survival are already offered by your backyard:

● Is there a continuous, although varying, food supply year-round?

● Is there a similar supply of water for drinking and bathing?

● Can birds make quick escapes from enemies, and roost protected from wind and rain or snow, in secure, sheltered plants?

● Can they find safe spots to successfully raise their young?

You may already have observed some answers to these questions through your living room window. Previous chapters of this book will help you to arrive at additional answers. Answer all four questions for every element of your existing backyard: every patch of weeds, every shrub, every tree, every major rise or fall in elevation.

If you can't identify a certain plant, stop your planning now and locate the necessary books and expertise to determine exactly what it is. You won't want to learn at some future time that you chopped down and discarded some beneficial, expensive plant in haste.

Keep track of all your answers on paper, both in words and on a map. The National Wildlife Federation offers an excellent set of tools for this task as part of its Gardening With Wildlife kit (Item No. 79907). For $19.95, plus $3.25 for shipping and handling, the kit offers several guides on backyard habitats, as well as grid paper and a landscape template. The template is a sheet of heavy plastic, with shapes that represent everything from evergreen trees to fence posts cut from it. For more information or to order the kit, write to the Federation at 1400 16th St., N.W., Washington, DC 20036 (Telephone: 800-432-6564).

To use grid paper for backyard mapping, assign a distance to be represented by each square of the grid. The Federation's paper suggests one-quarter inch, or two grid spaces, to represent one foot. At that scale a shrub that occupies three square feet would be represented on the map by a space of six grid squares by six grid squares.

LEFT Beautiful homes and beautiful backyards, but, like too much of modern suburbia, not much value for birds and other wildlife.

Draw your home on the map as your starting point. Add any sidewalks, patios, decks and the like. Finish it off with the outlines of existing plants. Leave lawn areas represented by blank spaces.

On a second piece of grid paper, adhering to the same scale, sketch in the existing elements that you plan to keep as part of your revised property. Start with your home. Finally, after all of these are shown, sketch the new elements that you plan to add, in their proposed locations. Everything that will be part of your new backyard should be shown when you are finished, down to the smallest nestbox or feeder. For seasonal items, such as suet or hummingbird feeders, use a dotted line.

Label every item as specifically as you can on the new map. If you definitely want honeysuckle in the northwest corner of

**RIGHT The National Wildlife Federation offers a kit that helps a homeowner to produce a professional-looking landscape plan for developing any backyard into a thriving wildlife habitat.**

the lot, label it as such. But if at this point you know only that you want that corner to be a thicket, and want to wait until after consulting with your nursery center to make specific choices, draw the outline of a few shrubs or a hedge and simply label it "thicket" for now.

With your plan in hand, visit one or more reliable nursery centers in your area. You may be surprised at the costs of

plants. What you've planned may take years to fit into your budget. Nonetheless, go over the entire plan with the experts. Get prices for every plant you planned into your habitat. Take notes on all their recommendations for substitutes that may be more beneficial to birds in your area, better able to survive and prosper in your area or more affordable. After this meeting, you may need to revise your plan into several one-year stages, each with its own map. Or, you may want to completely revise the plan from scratch.

Independent of any such changes, at all stages of planning try to achieve a year-round succession of food and shelter, rather than one burst in the spring or summer. Different plants that produce and hold their berries, fruits, seeds and foliage at different, but overlapping, times of the year will attract more birds and keep more of them in your backyard.

In trying to achieve all this diversity and balance, you must be careful to not become carried away with your planning. Too many plants scheduled too tightly into the space you have available could wreck your plans quickly. Consider each plant's height and breadth at maturity, not when it is planted.

Also, don't be too quick to do away with every last bit of lawn. You'll want ample open space to enjoy your new habitat, both watching it from a window and spending time outside in it. You may also want a vegetable garden, some space for the children to play and so on. Include this open

....................
**ABOVE In planning your backyard habitat, take some time to think like a bird. For example, glass windows and doors can appear to be open spaces to the birds, causing collisions like the one that left this powdery print of a mourning dove on a glass stormdoor.**
....................

ABOVE Edge, the place where
two distinct habitat types
meet, generally supports
more wildlife than either of
the habitat types alone. Here,
edge is formed where the open
lawn meets the briars and
where the briars meet the
woodland.

space now or you may not have room for it later. If your plans include relatively large expanses of thick shrubs and trees, add a pathway through them. Not only will this allow you access to all that you've created, but it will also provide a very valuable commodity in the natural world – edge.

## Some natural concepts

Edge is one of the most important concepts to anyone attempting to attract a wide variety of birds. It is created wherever two environments – lawn and hedgerow, for example – come together. Because of the mixing of elements from both converging environments, the edge generally will attract more wildlife and a wider variety than either of the two separate environments.

Clusters of plants scattered about the yard can maximize edge, as can a curving and meandering pattern for larger areas. Changes in elevation can provide a measure of edge. Abrupt changes, such as a stone wall between tiered levels, are of particular interest to birds because of the diversity of food they provide, both animal and vegetable.

A second concept of the natural world is that death is not the final stage for any part of the environment. In nature, death renders nothing useless and waiting to be discarded. Everything has additional uses beyond its life, including trees.

If you have dead or dying trees on your property, in such a spot that they won't pose a hazard, plan to keep them where they are. A large, rotting, partially hollow snag, with its ready abundance of insects and potential nesting cavities, attracts a great many birds that might otherwise avoid your yard.

Similarly, limbs and twigs trimmed from trees and shrubs will continue to attract birds if they are applied to a brush pile. A few layers of 4- to 6-foot-long logs, laid in an overlapping checkerboard pattern and covered with those limbs and branches, can be a magnet to small, thicket-loving birds.

Probably the most important concept, and the most difficult for all-conquering man to accept, is the simple fact that nature is ultimately in charge of everything in a new habitat. Plantings won't grow to maturity any faster than they've been naturally programmed to do so. And, whatever you do in your backyard, nature will change eventually. That's how fallow fields become forests, lakes become swamps and your backyard becomes a full-featured habitat beyond anything you might buy at the nursery.

# 6

# Reaping what you've sown

OPPOSITE What bird is that?
It's only natural to want to
know your birds, especially
when you've worked so hard to
develop the backyard habitat
that has attracted them. In this
photo, it's an eastern phoebe.

75

YOUR FEEDERS, baths and nestboxes are in place. Some fresh plantings are beginning to take hold. The birds are beginning to accept your backyard as part of their natural world. You've done what you can to benefit the birds, and they've accepted your offer. Now it's time for you to become the beneficiary of the birds.

Identification generally is the first concern of new birdwatchers. It's only natural to want to know your birds, especially when you've worked so hard to develop the backyard habitat that has attracted them.

## Field guide choices, uses

An easy-to-use field guide will be your first purchase for this effort. Some of the more respected names in field guides are Roger Tory Peterson, the Audubon Society, and the team of Chandler Robbins, Bertel Bruun and Herbert Zim. But, before you rush out and buy on name alone, spend some time watching the birds. Take notes describing them. After you've done this with a few species, compare your notes to determine trends in the way you observe the birds. Perhaps you will be able to locate a compatible field guide.

Page through several before making your choice. Some will be pocket-sized, intended for use in the field. Others will be much larger. If you're planning to use the field guide only from your window, size may not be a factor. Some will use photos to illustrate the birds. Others will use sketches or paintings. Good color portrait photos of birds are a relatively recent development, but they are quite popular. Some books will arrange the birds in their taxonomic families, while others will group them by size, shape or color. The latter is much easier for the beginning birdwatcher to use successfully.

After you have familiarized yourself with the field guide's organization, settle into your birdwatching spot and lay the field guide aside. Instead of frantically flipping through the book every time a bird happens by, for now concentrate on really seeing the bird.

Look for its field marks, which are characteristics such as color, shape or markings that can distinguish that bird in the field from similar species. Give yourself a systematic approach for noting them, such as starting at the head and working to the tail, and stick to it. Field marks include:

Size and shape of bill, tail and wings; a crest or lack of it on the head; eye rings or lines, which are markings around, above or through the eye; wing bars, which are one or two lines of contrasting color or shade running across the bird's wing; white patches on the wing, tail or rump that show when the bird is in flight; and general color pattern.

Note the size of the bird in comparison to common birds that you are already familiar with, such as the house sparrow, American robin, blue jay and common crow. Instead of trying to estimate the bird's size, simply note where it falls among these four.

Finally, note the bird's behavior: if it's traveling alone or in a flock; if it's eating and perching on the ground, in low shrubs or in tall trees; its motion when in flight; the habitat it chooses; and the time of year.

With all this information in mind, or jotted on a piece of paper, page through your field guide, looking for matches. Later, when you know the book like the back of your hand, you'll be able to turn quickly to the correct section on first spotting a bird. But for now you're better off building up a full mental picture of the bird rather than fruitlessly turning endless pages.

**OPPOSITE Now, it's time for you to be the beneficiary of the birds.**

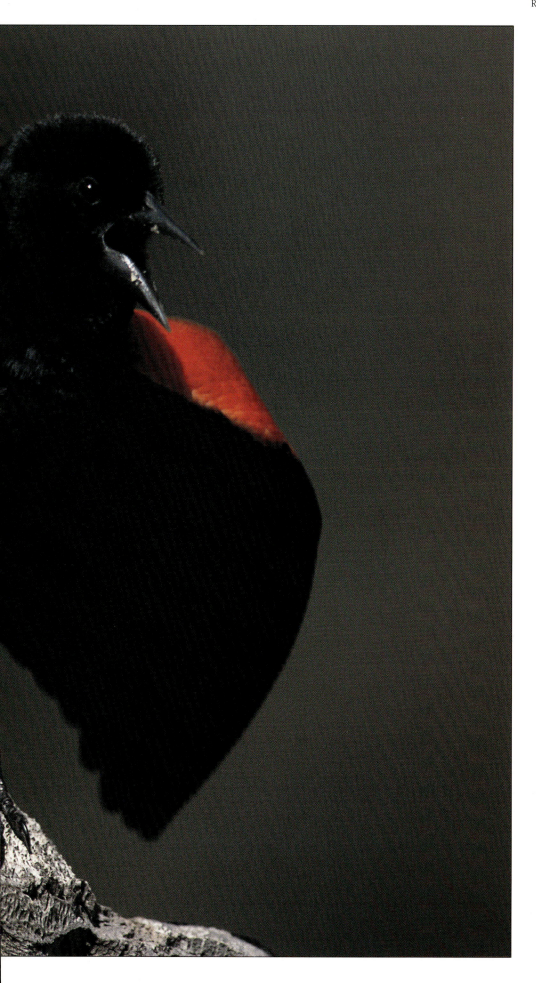

......................
**LEFT** Spend even a few
minutes watching the birds in
your backyard and you'll see
an incredible array of
behaviors. This is a territorial
display by a red-winged
blackbird.
......................

## A closer look

A well-made pair of binoculars will greatly increase your success and enjoyment in identification, and in birdwatching in general. However, choosing a superior pair among the dozens generally available at well-stocked outdoor shops can be a trying experience. You'll find a wide price range, of which the top may be out of the question and the bottom will leave you with a greatly inferior product.

First, take inventory of the price ranges at a few stores in your area. Select your own price range, within which you will compare features and craftsmanship of similar binoculars. Being certain to compare the same features, check the following aspects of all pairs that interest you:

● Power: the magnification rate of the pair of binoculars. Somewhere on the housing you'll find a set of numbers, such as 6×30 or 7×35. The first of these is the power. A pair of binoculars with a power of 7× magnifies whatever you look at seven times. Most backyard birdwatchers prefer 7× or 8×. Higher powers tend to magnify any movements of the user, offer darker images and are more difficult to focus on close objects.

● Objective lenses: the second number, after the ×, is the size of these lenses, through which light enters the binoculars. The larger this number, the more light-gathering capacity in the binoculars.

● Brightness: hold the binoculars at arm's length and look into the eyepieces. You will see a bright area, the exit pupil, which will vary from a pinhole to a large, bright circle. Larger exit pupils will offer brighter images. You also can learn the size of the exit pupil by dividing the size of the objective lens by the binoculars' power. For example, a 6×30 binocular has an exit pupil of 5 mm. Exit pupils of 2 to 4 mm are recommended for bright light situations, 4 or 5 for shaded areas and more than 5 for use at dawn or dusk.

● Lens coating: film-coated optics to reduce light reflection and glare within the lens. Hold the pair of binoculars under fluorescent light and look into the objective

**OPPOSITE Most birdwatchers seem to eventually become bird photographers. Here, noted wildlife photographer Leonard Lee Rue III uses his living room as a photo blind.**

**BELOW A bewildering selection of binoculars, each with its own special features, is available at any well-stocked outdoor shop.**

LEFT & OPPOSITE Bird photography can become a passion in and of itself, leading photographers to elaborate setups and new heights.

lenses. If they are purple or amber, they are coated. If they are white, they are not properly coated.

● Field of view: the width of the image you see through the binoculars. It is usually measured as the width in feet when viewed at 1,000 yards. Sometimes it will be imprinted on the housing as degrees. Simply multiply the degrees by 52.5 and you will have the field of view in feet. Wider fields make it easier to locate birds through the glasses.

● Price: an excellent indicator of the quality of all these features. Costs are substantial for the high quality optics and expert precision mounting required for a superior pair of binoculars that renders crisp images. The manufacturer passes these costs along to the customer.

● Focus: center-focus allows focusing on much closer objects than individual eyepiece-focus.

● Mechanical parts: they should operate smoothly.

## Keeping a journal

Even with top-notch field guides and binoculars, much of what you observe in the birds will be lost to you, unless you have a means for recording and storing it. A birdwatcher's journal is a private collection of observations and thoughts. A spiral-bound or loose-leaf notebook will function just fine. As with what you write in the journal, the binder is a matter of personal choice. Use whatever you're comfortable with. Similarly, evolve your own style and method of recording your observations.

A few items that generally appear in journal entries are date and time, habitat, temperature, wind speed and direction, cloud cover, the species of bird, field marks if you can't

identify it, behavior, vocalization (song or calls) and your comments on what you've witnessed. Whatever catches your attention should be journal subject.

Many new birdwatchers shy away from sketching in their journals, thinking they would be ashamed of the results. They may be missing the chance to gain a better understanding of the birds. Sketching will force a deeper look for details and, thus, increases an observer's skills.

They also often overlook indexing their journals. When a birdwatcher has filled only one or two journals from a couple months of observation, an index may seem like much extra work for little benefit. But, in a few years when a couple dozen journals are stacked on the shelf, making a comparison between a current entry and a relevant entry from a past volume will be difficult at best. Such comparisons, and the understanding that accompanies them, may be avoided because of the difficulty. The collection of observations would be so much handier and inviting if they had been indexed from the very first journal, updated weekly or monthly.

Indexing is best done outside the journal. Index cards offer an easily expanded and altered medium. The index can be as simple as a card for each species of bird observed, with the date of each observation written on it in chronological order. Under such a system, it's quick and easy to compare various observations about a species. For something more elaborate that will permit cross-species comparisons, cards for the different behaviors observed, plants used by the birds and so on can be added.

A transcribed sample entry from my own journal follows:

"I just saw anting for the first time. Near the barberry hedge, where a small anthill had started to form, a blue jay landed next to the hill, surveyed it for a couple minutes, and then plucked one of the ants with its beak. Craning its neck as far as possible and extending a wing forward until its tip touched the ground, the jay rubbed the ant along the underside of the wing tips. When it apparently had used up that ant, the jay plucked another, and then another. Finally, the bird shook itself a bit and flew from the yard.

I went to the anthill for a closer look at the jay's aftermath. A half-dozen crushed ants were scattered there, where the jay had been, apparently those he had used in his anting.

The books say that this behavior may have something to do with the bird using the acids that the crushed ants emit. One reference says it is formic acid, which has been shown to kill feather lice."

In addition to journals, many birdwatchers maintain lifelists, tallies of all the birds they've seen during their lives, when they've seen them and where. Yearlists, statelists and so

......................
**RIGHT A pair of male ring-necked pheasants wanders onto the lawn.**
......................

......................
**BELOW A multiple flash setup is used here to photograph hummingbirds.**
......................

on are variations of the lifelist. Some publishers even offer prepared lifelists, with all species for the continents already printed in them. The user simply makes his or her notes in the space provided. Like journals, the lists can provide handy joggers for pleasant memories. But they can also become all-consuming passions, driving birdwatchers relentlessly to rush to the scene of any reported sighting of any bird not yet ticked off on their lists. Somehow, that seems like something other than birdwatching.

To take the bird-recording a step further, you might want to take part in one or more of the organized bird feeder surveys conducted on a continuing basis. For the entire North American continent, there is project FeederWatch, which was

started in 1987 by the Cornell Laboratory of Ornithology, in New York, and the Long Point Bird Observatory, in Ontario. Volunteers are provided with computer-readable data forms to record their observations of birds at their feeders. Its first year, Project FeederWatch attracted nearly 4,000 participants to watch their feeders on one or two consecutive days of each week from November 14 through April 1. A total of 244 different species were recorded. These records provide information for a study of winter bird populations across the continent and their use of bird feeders. In return, the volunteers receive newsletters about bird feeding and analyses of the abundance and distribution of feeder birds across North America. Information about is available through

the Cornell Laboratory of Ornithology, Room 38, 159 Sapsucker Woods Road, Ithica, NY 14850.

Many states have similar programs. For example, the Nongame Program of the Iowa Department of Natural Resources – which, incidentally, uses a chickadee as its symbol – conducts its feeder survey a few days each January. Almost 1,000 individuals provided information during the 1988 survey. "The data gained from the survey is becoming increasingly useful for monitoring our winter birds and understanding why changes occur," Laura Spess Jackson of the Nongame Program explained in a recent newsletter. To learn if your state conducts such a program, contact your game or conservation agency.

## Smile and watch the birdie

At some point in your birdwatching career, you'll get the urge to record your feathered visitors on film. Perhaps you want to share your observations and relive memories with friends. Maybe you dream of seeing a photo you've shot on the cover of your favorite birdwatching magazine. Maybe you want the longer, more careful study of the birds that a photo affords.

If you're new to the world of photography, your first visit to the store can leave you awestruck. Counter after counter offer the latest high-tech wizardry. Cameras today are available in everything from point-and-shoot models that do everything except find a photogenic subject, to those with

complicated arrays of dials, knobs and buttons that all must be set manually to produce even a recognizable image.

A 35mm single lens reflex camera is the choice of most photographers today. It allows the subject to be viewed directly through the viewfinder, is lightweight and compact, and offers easy lens changing.

Much debate concerns the relative merits of manual and automatic camera systems. Manual requires the photographer to adjust all settings to capture the shot, while fully automatic asks the photographer only to frame his desired subject in the viewfinder and push the shutter release button. Some of the automatic systems produce excellent photos, but I would recommend buying a system that also allows fully manual operation. You may find that in time you want the option of creative control over every aspect of the process.

For this same reason, I would also recommend that you buy a camera that allows you to change lenses. Some of the point-and-shoot 35mm cameras do not offer this option. "Normal" lenses, supplied with many cameras, are in the range of 50mm or 55mm, which approximates normal eyesight. But, in bird photography, you'll eventually want to shoot close-ups of your subjects, or at least have them fill most of the frame. For this you will need to move impossibly close to the birds or use what is known as a telephoto lens. They accomplish much the same for the camera and film as a pair of binoculars does for the eyes. Every 50mm increase over the "normal" lens is equivalent to another power increase in the binoculars. For example, a 100mm lens offers roughly the same magnification as a 2× pair of binoculars, and a 400mm lens is equivalent to an 8× pair of binoculars.

Beyond these few basic principles, spend some time reading recent comparison articles in major photography magazines. The writers/testers are quite adept at ferreting out even the slightest qualitative and functional differences among comparable models.

Books abound on every aspect of photography, but one of the easiest to understand and most thorough on the specific topic of wildlife photography is *A Practical Guide to Photographing American Wildlife* by Joe McDonald, whose work illustrates some of the pages of the book you're now holding. His book will take you from a more in-depth understanding of photographic basics through the special needs of wildlife photography.

......................
**LEFT Of course, birds can bring a few special problems with them as well, like the penchant of some species and individuals to perch on washline posts. This is a female eastern bluebird.**
......................

87

# 7

## Some common backyard birds

OPPOSITE A male evening
grosbeak scrapes the tender
center from a berry.

89

MANY EXCELLENT books have been written on the identification of birds, their eggs and their nests. That's not the primary topic of this chapter. The following listings will help you to get started in the identification of some of the more common backyard visitors/residents. But the main subject, here, is how to attract those birds.

Each listing is composed in the following manner:

## COMMON NAME OF BIRD
### SCIENTIFIC NAME

IDENTIFICATION: approximate size range in inches (size range in centimeters, rounded to whole numbers); field comparison on the house sparrow-American robin-blue jay-common crow scale; description, concentrating on quickly identifiable field marks.

NESTING: number of eggs, description of nest, where the nest is built.

HABITAT: specifics, such as thickets, and more general, such as residential areas.

RANGE: breeding; winter.

FEEDER FOODS: (type of feeder) alphabetical listing of some feeder foods that have been successful with this bird.

ATTRACTIVE PLANTINGS: (general techniques, such as ground cover) alphabetical listing of individual species, and sometimes families, of plants that have been successful with this bird.

Use the listings as a starting point, not the absolute final words, on what will bring a particular bird into your backyard. The suggestions have proven successful for other backyard birdwatchers, but your own experimentation is certain to find new feeder techniques, feeder foods and plantings that will be the perfect attractors for your backyard. Such experimentation is the real spice of backyard bird feeding and habitat building. Rest assured that if you hit on the correct combinations, the birds will reward your efforts.

**KEY**

**A** BREEDING RANGE

**B** WINTERING RANGE

OPPOSITE Evening grosbeaks add a spark of brilliance to the backyard, but even a small flock can eat a great deal of seed in a relatively short time.

## AMERICAN GOLDFINCH
### CARDUELIS TRISTIS

**IDENTIFICATION:** 4½ to 5½ inches (11-14 cm); smaller than a sparrow; male, spring and summer, bright yellow, black forehead, wings and tail, with white rump and wing edges; female and winter male, duller, grayer, black wings and tail, white wing bars.

**NESTING:** 4 to 6 blue eggs in cup of grass, bark strips and plant down, in fork of sapling or shrub.

**HABITAT:** residential areas, thickets, weedy grasslands with trees.

**RANGE:** breeds from southern Canada south into California and South Carolina; winters in most of U.S.

**FEEDER FOODS:** hulled sunflower seeds, niger seeds, oil-type sunflower seeds.

**ATTRACTIVE PLANTINGS:** alder, American hornbeam, bachelor's buttons, birch, cosmos, elm, hemlock, lambsquarter, panic grasses, ragweed, spruce, sunflower, sycamore, zinnia.

## AMERICAN ROBIN
### TURDUS MIGRATORIUS

**IDENTIFICATION:** 9 to 11 inches (23-28 cm); gray above, orange-red below, black head and tail

**NESTING:** 3 to 5 "robin's egg blue" eggs in cup of grass and twigs reinforced with mud and lined with softer grasses, in a tree or on ledge.

**HABITAT:** farmlands, residential areas, woodlands.

**RANGE:** breeds across entire continent, except extreme north; winters south of U. S.-Canadian border.

**FEEDER FOODS:** (not much of a feeder bird) apple bits, bread, raisins.

**ATTRACTIVE PLANTINGS:** arbutis, barberry, bayberry, beauty berry, bittersweet, black gum, cherry, cotoneaster, crabapple, currant, date palm, dogwood, elderberry, hawthorn, honeysuckle, juniper, mountain ash, mulberry, persimmon, Russian olive, sumac, snowberry, Virginia creeper, yew.

## BARN SWALLOW
### HIRUNDO RUSTICA

**IDENTIFICATION:** 7 inches (18cm); between sparrow and robin; iridescent blue above, buff below, long forked tail.

**NESTING:** 3 to 6 white eggs spotted brown in straw, weed and mud nest lined with feathers, inside outbuildings.

**HABITAT:** farmland, ranches, semi-woodlands, all near water.

**RANGE:** breeds from Alaska and northern Alberta east to Nova Scotia and south throughout most of U.S.; winters in South America.

**FEEDER FOODS:**–

**ATTRACTIVE PLANTINGS:** (insects) lawn.

## BLACK-CAPPED CHICKADEE
### PARUS ATRICAPILLUS

**IDENTIFICATION:** 4¾ to 5¾ inches (12-15cm); smaller than a sparrow; gray back, whitish underparts, black cap and throat, white cheeks.

**NESTING:** 5 to 10 white eggs spotted brown in cup of grass, plant down, moss and fur, in cavity.

**HABITAT:** mixed woodlands, winters in residential areas.

**RANGE:** breeds from Alaska and British Columbia east to New-foundland and south to California and New Jersey; winters throughout breeding range and a few hundred miles further south.

**FEEDER FOODS:** (hanging, pole and ground feeders) oil-type sunflower seeds.

**ATTRACTIVE PLANTINGS:** blueberry, elm, fir, hemlock, oak, pine, salal, serviceberry, spruce, sweet gum, sycamore, Virginia creeper.

## BLACK-CHINNED HUMMINGBIRD

ARCHILOCHUS ALEXANDRI

**IDENTIFICATION:** 3¼ to 3¾ inches (8-10 cm); smaller than a sparrow; green above, white below; male, black throat and cheeks, violet lower throat; female, whitish throat.

**NESTING:** 2 tiny white eggs in cup, in shrub or tree.

**HABITAT:** canyons, chaparral, residential areas in foothills.

**RANGE:** breeds from British Columbia south throughout the western U. S., except the Pacific Northwest, to Mexico; winters south of the U.S.-Mexican border.

**FEEDER FOODS:** (hummingbird feeder) sugar-water solution.

**ATTRACTIVE PLANTINGS:** azalea, bellflower, bouncing betty, canna, century plant, coral bells, day lily, erythrina, flowering tobacco, foxglove, gladiolus, hollyhock, jasmines, larkspur, lily, matrimony vine, mint, morning glory, painted cup, penstemon, phlox, poppy, rattlesnake root, sweet william, trumpet creeper.

## BLUE JAY

CYANOCITTA CRISTATA

**IDENTIFICATION:** 12 inches (30 cm); bright blue above, white below, white and black in blue wing, black facial marks, crest.

**NESTING:** 3 to 6 olive eggs spotted brown in coarse bowl of thorny sticks and leaves lined with grass and rootlets, in fork of tree.

**HABITAT:** city parks, oak forests, residential areas.

**RANGE:** breeds and winters from Manitoba and Newfoundland south to Texas and Florida, all east of the Rocky Mountains.

**FEEDER FOODS:** (ground, pole, hanging and suet feeders) cracked corn, fresh fruit bits, oil-type sunflower seeds, suet.

**ATTRACTIVE PLANTINGS:** beech, cherry, Douglas fir, elm, grape, hawthorn, hemlock, huckleberry, juniper, mulberry, oak, pine, plum, spruce.

## BREWER'S BLACKBIRD

EUPHAGUS CYANOCEPHALUS

**IDENTIFICATION:** 8 to 10 inches (20-25 cm); robin size; male, black, iridescent purple head, yellow eyes; female, gray, dark eyes.

**NESTING:** 3 to 5 gray eggs spotted brown in coarse nest of twigs and grass lined with softer grass and hair, on or near ground.

**HABITAT:** farmlands.

**RANGE:** breeds from British Columbia and Manitoba south throughout central and western U.S.; winters south of the U.S.-Canadian border.

**FEEDER FOODS:** (ground feeder) cracked corn, white proso millet.

**ATTRACTIVE PLANTINGS:**—

## BROWN-HEADED COWBIRD

MOLOTHRUS ATER

**IDENTIFICATION:** 6 to 8 inches (15-20 cm); between sparrow and robin; gray, male has glossy brown head, conical bill.

**NESTING:** 1 white egg speckled with brown in nest of some other bird species, 4 or 5 eggs laid in total in same number of nests.

**HABITAT:** farmlands, residential areas, woodland edge.

**RANGE:** breeds from southern Canada throughout U.S.; winters in southern U.S.

**FEEDER FOODS:** (ground feeder) bread, cracked corn, table scraps.

**ATTRACTIVE PLANTINGS:** lawn.

## BROWN THRASHER

TOXOSTOMA RUFUM

**IDENTIFICATION:** 10½ to 12 inches (27-30 cm); blue jay size; brown above, white with brown streaks below, long tail, curved bill.

**NESTING:** 4 or 5 blue eggs with brown dots in coarse nest of twigs and leaves lined with grass, near the ground in thorny shrub.

**HABITAT:** overgrown fields, thickets, woodland edge.

**RANGE:** breeds from southern Canada south to Texas and Florida; winters from Texas east to Florida and along Atlantic Coast; all east of the Rocky Mountains.

**FEEDER FOODS:** (ground feeder) bread, raisins, walnut meats.

**ATTRACTIVE PLANTINGS:** (thickets with leaf mulch beneath them) autumn olive, beauty berry, cherry, crabapple, dogwood, elderberry, honeysuckle, mountain ash, plum, pokeberry, strawberry, sumac.

## BUSHTIT

PSALTRIPARUS MINIMUS

**IDENTIFICATION:** 3¾ to 4¼ inches (9-11 cm); smaller than a sparrow; gray back, whitish underparts, gray crown, brown cheeks, short bill, long tail.

**NESTING:** 5 to 7 white eggs in long, woven pouch, in shrub or tree.

**HABITAT:** chaparral, mixed woodlands, oak scrub.

**RANGE:** breeds and winters in southwestern Canada south and east as far as Oklahoma.

**FEEDER FOODS:**–

**ATTRACTIVE PLANTINGS:** wild lilac.

## CAROLINA CHICKADEE

PARUS CAROLINENSIS

**IDENTIFICATION:** 4 to 5 inches (10-13 cm); smaller than a sparrow; gray above, white below, black cap and throat, white cheeks.

**NESTING:** 5 to 8 white eggs spotted brown in cup lined with feathers and plant down, in cavity.

**HABITAT:** deciduous woodlands, residential areas.

**RANGE:** breeds and winters from New Jersey, Ohio and Oklahoma south throughout U.S.

**FEEDER FOODS:** (hanging, pole, ground and suet feeders) bone with meat and gristle on it, bread, cheese, nut kernels, oil-type sunflower seeds, peanut butter, pumpkin seeds, suet.

**ATTRACTIVE PLANTINGS:** fir, hemlock, pines, salal, spruce, sycamore.

## CEDAR WAXING

BOMBYCILLA CEDRORUM

**IDENTIFICATION:** 6½ to 8 inches (16-20 cm); between sparrow and robin; brown above, olive-yellow below, black mask, yellow tail tip, red tips on secondary wing feathers, crest.

**NESTING:** 4 to 6 blue eggs spotted brown and black in cup of grass and twigs, in tree.

**HABITAT:** farmlands with trees, residential areas, woodlands.

**RANGE:** breeds from southern Canada south into mid-U.S.; winters south of U.S.-Canadian border.

**FEEDER FOODS:**–

**ATTRACTIVE PLANTINGS:** American bittersweet, arbutis, cherry, Chinese elm, choke cherry, cotoneaster, date palm, firethorn, hawthorn, honeysuckle, juniper, mountain ash, persimmon, privet, serviceberry, snowberry, viburnum.

## CHIMNEY SWIFT
CHAETURA PELAGICA

**IDENTIFICATION:** 4¾ to 5½ inches (12-14 cm); small sparrow size; brown-gray, short body, short tail, long wings.

**NESTING:** 3 to 6 white eggs in half-saucer of twigs bound by bird's saliva, attached to inside wall of chimney, cave or hollow tree.

**HABITAT:** chimneys, the sky.

**RANGE:** breeds from southern Saskatchewan and Nova Scotia south through the Gulf Coast; winters in South America.

**FEEDER FOODS:**—

**ATTRACTIVE PLANTINGS:** (insects) lawn.

## CHIPPING SPARROW
SPIZELLA PASSERINA

**IDENTIFICATION:** 5 to 5¾ inches (13-14 cm); small sparrow; brown and black streaks above, gray below, gray cheeks and rump, brown crown, white eyebrow, black eyeline.

**NESTING:** 3 to 5 pale blue eggs in cup of grass, almost always lined with hair, in shrub or vine tangle.

**HABITAT:** city parks, pastures, residential areas, woodland edge.

**RANGE:** breeds throughout entire continent, except northernmost areas; winters in southeast U.S.

**FEEDER FOODS:** (ground feeder) black-stripe sunflower seeds, cracked corn, suet.

**ATTRACTIVE PLANTINGS:** (rose thickets) phlox, pines, vines, zinnia.

## CLIFF SWALLOW
PETROCHELIDON PYRRHONOTA

**IDENTIFICATION:** 5 to 6 inches (13-15 cm); sparrow size; blue above, white below, white forehead, brown throat, buff rump, square tail.

**NESTING:** 3 to 6 white eggs spotted red-brown in gourd-shaped hollow made of mud pellets on buildings, bridges and cliffs.

**HABITAT:** canyons, cliffs, farmlands, meadows.

**RANGE:** breeds from southern Canada south into central America; winters in South America.

**FEEDER FOODS:**—

**ATTRACTIVE PLANTINGS:**—

## COMMON CROW
CORVUS BRACHYRHYNCHOS

**IDENTIFICATION:** 17 to 21 inches (43-53 cm); all black, stocky body, stout bill, fan-shaped tail.

**NESTING:** 4 to 6 gray-green eggs spotted brown and dark gray in large basket of twigs, vines and sticks with lining of feathers, grass, fur, shredded bark and rootlets, in top of a tall tree.

**HABITAT:** farmlands, residential areas, woodlands.

**RANGE:** breeds from southern two-thirds of Canada south throughout U.S.; winters south of the U.S.-Canadian border.

**FEEDER FOODS:** (ground feeder) bread, corn, table scraps.

**ATTRACTIVE PLANTINGS:** Tall trees, open lawn.

95

## COMMON FLICKER

COLAPTES AURATUS

**IDENTIFICATION:** 12 to 13 inches (30-33 cm); blue jay size; brown back with black spots, white below with black spots and black bib, gray nape and crown with red patch, light brown face with black cheek patch.

**NESTING:** 3 to 10 white eggs, in cavity.

**HABITAT:** city parks, farmland with trees, residential areas.

**RANGE:** breeds from Newfoundland and Manitoba south to the Gulf Coast; winters from southern Canada into Mexico.

**FEEDER FOODS:** (ground, hanging, pole and suet feeders) black-stripe sunflower seeds, peanut butter, suet.

**ATTRACTIVE PLANTINGS:** blackberry, black gum, blueberry, cherry, dogwood, grape, greenbrier, hackberry, hawthorn, honeysuckle, mountain ash, mulberry, serviceberry, Virginia creeper.

## COMMON GRACKLE

QUISCALUS QUISCULA

**IDENTIFICATION:** 11 to 13½ inches (28-34 cm); blue jay size; all black (at distance), iridescent colors from blue to bronze (close up), bright yellow eyes, long wedge-shaped tail.

**NESTING:** 3 to 6 blue eggs spotted brown in mass of twigs lined with grass and feathers, in tree.

**HABITAT:** cities, fields, residential areas, woodlands.

**RANGE:** breeds from northern Alberta and Nova Scotia south throughout U.S., east of Rocky Mountains; winters south of U.S.-Canadian border.

**FEEDER FOODS:** (suet and ground feeders) black-stripe sunflower seeds, bread, cracked corn, suet, table scraps.

**ATTRACTIVE PLANTINGS:** conifers, lawn.

## DARK-EYED JUNCO

JUNCO HYEMALIS

**IDENTIFICATION:** 5½ to 6½ inches (14-16 cm); size of sparrow; slate-gray above, gray breast, white abdomen, pink bill.

**NESTING:** 3 to 5 pale green eggs with brown spots in deep cup of moss, grass and bark strips, near or on ground, particularly in a bank.

**HABITAT:** forests; winters in fields, backyards, parks.

**RANGE:** breeds from Alaska and Newfoundland south into western U.S. and along Appalachian Mountains into Georgia; winters south of the U.S.-Canadian border.

**FEEDER FOODS:** (ground feeder) bread crumbs, grains, peanut butter, suet, sunflower seeds, walnut meats.

**ATTRACTIVE PLANTINGS:** sweet birch.

## DOWNY WOODPECKER

PICOIDES PUBESCENS

**IDENTIFICATION:** 6 to 7 inches (15-18 cm); sparrow size; black and white spotted above, gray-white below, male has red patch on nape.

**NESTING:** 3 to 6 white eggs on sawdust, in cavity.

**HABITAT:** parks, small woodlands, residential areas.

**RANGE:** breeds from Alaska through southern Canada south throughout U.S., except southwest region; winters in same range.

**FEEDER FOODS:** (suet and pole feeders) black-stripe sunflower seeds, crumbled doughnuts, peanut butter, suet.

**ATTRACTIVE PLANTINGS:** (dead, mature trees) cherry, dogwood, mulberry, oak, spruce, sumac, viburnum, Virginia creeper.

## EASTERN BLUEBIRD
### SIALIA SIALIS

**IDENTIFICATION:** 6½ to 7½ inches (16-19 cm); between sparrow and robin; bright blue above, red-brown breast, white belly, female slightly duller.

**NESTING:** 3 to 6 blue eggs in cup of grass and plant stem, in cavity.

**HABITAT:** farmlands.

**RANGE:** breeds from southern Canada south into Texas and Florida; winters south of the Great Lakes; all east of the Great Plains.

**FEEDER FOODS:**—

**ATTRACTIVE PLANTINGS:** (snags) American bittersweet, autumn olive, black gum, camphor, cherry, date palm, dogwood, elderberry, holly, honeysuckle, mountain ash, persimmon, pokeberry, sumac, viburnum.

## EASTERN KINGBIRD
### TYRANNUS TYRANNUS

**IDENTIFICATION:** 8 to 9 inches (20-23 cm); small robin size; dark gray above, white below, black on head, black tail with white tip, concealed red crown patch.

**NESTING:** 3 to 5 cream eggs spotted brown and black in stick nest lined with grass, in shrub or tree.

**HABITAT:** farms, open country.

**RANGE:** breeds from Alberta and Newfoundland south throughout U.S., except West Coast, southwest region and southwest Texas; winters in South America.

**FEEDER FOODS:**—

**ATTRACTIVE PLANTINGS:** cherry.

## EASTERN PHOEBE
### SAYORNIS PHOEBE

**IDENTIFICATION:** 6¼ to 7¼ inches (15-18 cm); bigger than sparrow, smaller than robin; olive-green above, buff-gray below.

**NESTING:** 3 to 6 white eggs in grass and mud bowl lined with hair and moss, attached to building ledges, cliffs, bridges.

**HABITAT:** buildings with ledges, woodlands near streams.

**RANGE:** breeds from northern Manitoba south through Texas, northern Quebec south through the Carolinas; winters in southeast U.S.; all east of the Rocky Mountains.

**FEEDER FOODS:** berries (in absence of insects)

**ATTRACTIVE PLANTINGS:** juniper.

## EUROPEAN STARLING
### STURNUS VULGARIS

**IDENTIFICATION:** 7½ to 8½ inches (19-21 cm); between sparrow and robin; iridescent black (white flecks in winter), short tail, stocky, long bill, yellow bill in summer, dark bill in winter.

**NESTING:** 4 to 6 blue eggs in nest of twigs and debris lined with fine plant fibers and feathers, in cavity.

**HABITAT:** cities, farmlands, residential areas.

**RANGE:** breeds and winters from southern Alaska and southern Canada south through entire U.S.

**FEEDER FOODS:** (ground feeder) bread, cracked corn, table scraps.

**ATTRACTIVE PLANTINGS:** lawn.

ABOVE The blue jay is a
common visitor to the
backyard; one of the boldest
species, it has fully adapted to
living with people.

## FOX SPARROW

PASSERELLA ILIACA

**IDENTIFICATION:** 6½ to 7½ inches (16-19 cm); large sparrow; striped gray-brown and black above, white below with brown spots, head gray with brown stripes.

**NESTING:** 3 to 5 pale green eggs spotted brown in cup of leaves, grass and moss, on or near ground.

**HABITAT:** coniferous woodland, winters in weedy pastures and roadside thickets.

**RANGE:** breeds from Alaska and northern Quebec south to northern U.S.; winters south to the Gulf Coast.

**FEEDER FOODS:** (ground feeder) black-stripe sunflower seeds, white proso millet.

**ATTRACTIVE PLANTINGS:** (hedgerows with leaf litter beneath them, thickets) hawthorn, phlox, zinnia.

## GRAY CATBIRD

DUMETELLA CAROLINENSIS

**IDENTIFICATION:** 8 to 9¼ inches (20-23 cm); smaller than a robin; slender body, long tail, dark gray, black cap, rusty under tail.

**NESTING:** 2 to 5 blue-green eggs in mass of twigs and leaves lined with softer plant fibers, in dense shrub or vine tangle.

**HABITAT:** residential areas and thickets.

**RANGE:** breeds from southern Canada south into Florida and Texas; winters in southern United States into Central America.

**FEEDER FOODS:** apples, bread, cheese, cherries, currants, grapes, oranges, peanuts, raisins.

**ATTRACTIVE PLANTINGS:** American bittersweet, beauty berry, buckthorn, cherry, greenbrier, mountain ash, strawberry, viburnum, Virginia creeper.

## HAIRY WOODPECKER

PICOIDES VILLOSUS

**IDENTIFICATION:** 8½ to 10½ inches (21-27 cm); robin size; black and white, unspotted white back, long bill, male has red head patch.

**NESTING:** 3 to 6 white eggs, in cavity.

**HABITAT:** deciduous forest, winter range includes residential areas.

**RANGE:** breeds and winters from Alaska and most of Canada south throughout U.S.

**FEEDER FOODS:** (suet, hanging and pole feeders) black-stripe sunflower seeds, suet.

**ATTRACTIVE PLANTINGS:** (dead, mature trees) cherry, oak, viburnum.

## HOUSE FINCH

CARPODACUS MEXICANUS

**IDENTIFICATION:** 5 to 6 inches (13-15 cm); sparrow size; male, streaked brown, red breast, forehead and rump; female, streaked brown.

**NESTING:** 2 to 6 pale blue eggs spotted black in cup of grass, in thicket or cavity or on house.

**HABITAT:** residential areas.

**RANGE:** breeds and winters from southern Quebec and Ontario south through Georgia, southern British Columbia south to the U.S.-Mexican border, absent from central and Gulf Coast U.S.

**FEEDER FOODS:** (hanging, pole and ground feeders) bread, fresh fruit bits, niger seeds, oil-type sunflower seeds, white proso millet.

**ATTRACTIVE PLANTINGS:** American bittersweet, ash, aspen, cotoneaster, currant, dogwood, elderberry, elm, honeysuckle, lilac, marigold, nasturtium, phlox, pines, snowberry, sycamore, willow, zinnia.

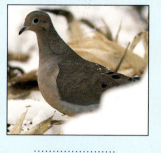

## HOUSE SPARROW
PASSER DOMESTICUS

**IDENTIFICATION:** 5 to 6½ inches (13-16 cm); male, black throat, white cheeks, brown nape, gray crown and rump; female, streaked brown above, dull white below, pale eyebrow.

**NESTING:** 3 to 7 white eggs speckled with brown in loose nest of grass and any debris available, in cavity.

**HABITAT:** always close to man.

**RANGE:** breeds and winters throughout southern Canada and entire U.S.

**FEEDER FOODS:** canary seeds, cracked corn, golden millet, white proso millet.

**ATTRACTIVE PLANTINGS:** American bittersweet, phlox, pine, zinnia.

## HOUSE WREN
TROGLODYTES AEDON

**IDENTIFICATION:** 4½ to 5¼ inches (11-13 cm); smaller than a sparrow; dusky brown above, pale below.

**NESTING:** 5 to 8 white eggs speckled with brown in cup of grass and sticks lined with feathers and soft material, in nesting cavity.

**HABITAT:** city parks, farmlands, residential areas, woodlands.

**RANGE:** breeds from British Columbia and southern Newfoundland south through California and South Carolina; winters in southeast U.S. and along Gulf Coast.

**FEEDER FOODS:** (not a feeder bird) maybe bug zapper feeder.

**ATTRACTIVE PLANTINGS:** (dead, mature trees).

## MOCKINGBIRD
MIMUS POLYGLOTTOS

**IDENTIFICATION:** 9 to 11 inches (23-28 cm); robin size; gray with white patches on wings and tail, slender, long tail.

**NESTING:** 3 to 5 blue-green eggs spotted brown in cup of sticks and weed stems, in thorny shrub or low tree.

**HABITAT:** city parks, farmlands, residential areas, thickets.

**RANGE:** breeds throughout U.S., except northwest region and Maine through northern New York; winters in Mid-Atlantic through southeast U.S. and southern California.

**FEEDER FOODS:** (suet, hanging and pole feeders) bread, currants, dried fruit bits, figs, nut meats, peanut butter, raisins, suet.

**ATTRACTIVE PLANTINGS:** (thickets, hedgerows) American bittersweet, barberry, beauty berry, blackberry, buckthorn, cherry, cotoneaster, crabapple, elderberry, firethorn, grape, greenbrier, holly, honeysuckle, mulberry, privet, red cedar, serviceberry, viburnum, Virginia creeper, yew.

## MOURNING DOVE
ZENAIDA MACROURA

**IDENTIFICATION:** 12 inches (30 cm); blue jay size; gray-brown above with black spots on wings, cream head with noticeable black eye, cream below, small head, pointed tail.

**NESTING:** 2 to 4 white eggs in loose nest of twigs in low shrubs or tall trees.

**HABITAT:** farmlands, parks, residential areas.

**RANGE:** breeds from southern Alaska and southern Canada throughout U.S.; winters south of U.S.-Canadian border.

**FEEDER FOODS:** (ground feeder) cracked corn, millet, oil-type sunflower seeds.

**ATTRACTIVE PLANTINGS:** conifers, pokeberry.

## NORTHERN CARDINAL
CARDINALIS CARDINALIS

**IDENTIFICATION:** 8 to 9 inches (20-23 cm); small robin size; male, brilliant red, black face, short red bill, crest; female, buff, red tinge on crest, wings and tail.

**NESTING:** 2 to 5 pale green eggs spotted brown in cup of twigs and plant fibers, in thicket.

**HABITAT:** residential areas, swamps, thickets, woodland edge.

**RANGE:** breeds and winters from Dakotas east to Nova Scotia and south to the Gulf Coast and in southern California-Arizona.

**FEEDER FOODS:** (hanging and ground feeders) black-stripe sunflower seeds, oil-type sunflower seeds, raisins, squash seeds.

**ATTRACTIVE PLANTINGS:** (hedgerows, thickets) American hornbeam, beauty berry, dogwood, elm, greenbrier, hackberry, mulberry, raspberry, rose, serviceberry, sumac, tulip tree, viburnum, Virginia creeper.

## NORTHERN ORIOLE
ICTERUS GALBULA

**IDENTIFICATION:** 7 to 8½ inches (18-21 cm); between sparrow and robin; male, black head, tail and wings, orange breast, rump and shoulder; female, olive above, dull orange below, dull white wing bars.

**NESTING:** 4 to 6 gray eggs spotted brown and black in sack of plant fibers, bark and string, hung from tip of a branch.

**HABITAT:** woodlands.

**RANGE:** breeds from south central Canada south throughout U.S., except southeast U.S.; winters in the tropics.

**FEEDER FOODS:** (suet and hanging feeders) berries, fresh fruit bits, grapes, nut meats, orange segments, raw ground beef, suet.

**ATTRACTIVE PLANTINGS:** birch, elm, mountain ash, sycamore.

## PINE SISKIN
CARDUELIS PINUS

**IDENTIFICATION:** 4½ to 5¼ inches (11-13 cm); smaller than a sparrow; heavily streaked brown with yellow in wings and tail, white wing bars.

**NESTING:** 3 to 6 green-blue eggs spotted brown in saucer of twigs and grass, in conifer.

**HABITAT:** mixed woodlands, residential areas, swamps.

**RANGE:** breeds from southern Manitoba and Nova Scotia south through northern U.S. and along Appalachian Mountains into North Carolina; winters south to Florida and Texas.

**FEEDER FOODS:** (hanging feeder) ashes, millet, melon and squash seeds, niger seeds, sunflower seeds.

**ATTRACTIVE PLANTINGS:** alder, birch, elm, hemlock.

## PURPLE FINCH
CARPODACUS PURPUREUS

**IDENTIFICATION:** 5½ to 6½ inches (14-16 cm); sparrow size; male, raspberry; female, streaked brown, bold eyebrow.

**NESTING:** 3 to 5 blue-green eggs spotted brown in cup of twigs and grass lined with hair, in conifer.

**HABITAT:** residential areas with conifers, woodlands.

**RANGE:** breeds from Newfoundland and Quebec south to New Jersey and the Great Lakes region of the U.S.; winters from Nova Scotia south to Florida and Texas.

**FEEDER FOODS:** (hanging feeder) black-stripe sunflower seeds, oil-type sunflower seeds.

**ATTRACTIVE PLANTINGS:** ash, aspen, conifers, cotoneaster, dogwood, elm, hawthorn, hemlock, phlox, spruce, sycamore, tulip tree, zinnia.

## PURPLE MARTIN

PROGNE SUBIS

**IDENTIFICATION:** 7 to 8½ inches (18-21 cm); between sparrow and robin; male, dark blue; female, duller above, gray below.

**NESTING:** 3 to 8 white eggs in mass of grass, leaves, paper and string, in cavity, usually a martin house.

**HABITAT:** farmlands, residential areas, woodlands.

**RANGE:** breeds from eastern British Columbia and southern Ontario and Quebec south throughout U.S.; winters in South America.

**FEEDER FOODS:**–

**ATTRACTIVE PLANTINGS:** lawns.

## RED-BELLIED WOODPECKER

CENTURUS CAROLINUS

**IDENTIFICATION:** 10 inches (25 cm); robin size; barred white and black above, buff below, red patch on lower abdomen, male has dull red crown and nape, female has dull red nape.

**NESTING:** 3 to 8 white eggs, in cavity.

**HABITAT:** woodlands, winter range includes residential areas.

**RANGE:** breeds and winters along U.S. Atlantic Coast west to Texas.

**FEEDER FOODS:** (suet feeder) suet.

**ATTRACTIVE PLANTINGS:** (dead, mature trees) cherry, oak, viburnum.

## RED-BREASTED NUTHATCH

SITTA CANADENSIS

**IDENTIFICATION:** 4½ to 4¾ inches (11-13 cm); smaller than a sparrow; black eyeline; male, black cap, white eyebrow, blue-gray above, reddish below; female, paler.

**NESTING:** 4 to 7 white eggs spotted brown, in conifer cavity.

**HABITAT:** conifer woodlands.

**RANGE:** breeds from British Columbia and Newfoundland south through southern California, the Great Lakes region, New Jersey and the Appalachian Mountains into North Carolina; winters over same region and throughout U.S.

**FEEDER FOODS:** (hanging feeder and pole feeder) black-stripe sunflower seeds, nut kernels, rotten apples.

**ATTRACTIVE PLANTINGS:** fir, maple, oak, spruce, sycamore.

## RED-WINGED BLACKBIRD

AGELAIUS PHOENICEUS

**IDENTIFICATION:** 7 to 9½ inches (17-24 cm); between sparrow and small robin; male, black, crimson shoulder patches; female, streaked brown.

**NESTING:** 3 to 5 pale blue eggs spotted brown and purple in cup of grass and reeds, on stout marsh plant or shrub in marsh.

**HABITAT:** meadows, swamps.

**RANGE:** breeds from southern Alaska, northern Manitoba and Newfoundland south through entire U.S.; winters in southern two-thirds of U.S. and northwest region of U.S.

**FEEDER FOODS:** (ground and suet feeders) cracked corn, dry dog food, hemp, millet, suet.

**ATTRACTIVE PLANTINGS:** (marshy area with reeds and similar wetland plants).

## RING-NECKED PHEASANT
### PHASIANUS COLCHICUS

**IDENTIFICATION:** 21 to 36 inches (53-91 cm); larger than a crow; chickenlike, long sweeping tail; male, shades of brown, gray and white on body, white neck ring, scarlet wattles, iridescent head colors; female, streaked shades of brown.

**NESTING:** 6 to 15 olive-brown eggs in depression lined with grass and weeds, on ground in tall grass.

**HABITAT:** farmlands, forest-field edge.

**RANGE:** breeds and winters throughout southern Canada, northeast U.S., the Great Lakes region and the Midwest.

**FEEDER FOODS:** (ground feeder) cracked corn, corn on cob.

**ATTRACTIVE PLANTINGS:** low conifers and hedgerows.

## RUBY-THROATED HUMMINGBIRD
### ARCHILOCHUS COLUBRIS

**IDENTIFICATION:** 3½ inches (9 cm); much smaller than a sparrow; metallic green above, white below, shimmering red throat on male, needlelike bill.

**NESTING:** 2 tiny white eggs in nest woven of plant down and spider silk, saddled to tree branch, covered with lichens.

**HABITAT:** parks, residential areas, woodlands.

**RANGE:** breeds from central Alberta through Newfoundland south throughout eastern half of U.S.; winters in Mexico and further south.

**FEEDER FOODS:** (hummingbird feeder) sugar-water in tube.

**ATTRACTIVE PLANTINGS:** bee balm, blue bell, butterfly bush, cardinal flower, columbine, cornflower, delphinium, figwort, four o'clock, fuchsia, hamelia, iris, jewelweed, lilac, lousewort, milkweed, monkey flower, nasturtium, pelargonium, petunia, poinciana, ragged robin, scabious, snapdragon, spiderflower, torch lilly.

## RUFOUS-SIDED TOWHEE
### PIPILO ERYTHROPHTHALMUS

**IDENTIFICATION:** 7 to 9½ inches (18-24 cm); between sparrow and robin; male, black above and head, white below, rufous patches on flanks; female, brown where male black.

**NESTING:** 4 to 6 white eggs spotted brown in cup of plant stems and grass, on or near ground.

**HABITAT:** thickets, woodland edge.

**RANGE:** breeds from south central Canada south throughout U.S., except the Great Plains; winters in the southern two-thirds of the U.S.

**FEEDER FOODS:** (ground feeder) bread, cracked corn, grains, nut kernels, peanuts.

**ATTRACTIVE PLANTINGS:** (ground covers, thickets) bayberry, blackberry, blueberry, holly, oak, pine, pokeberry, raspberry, serviceberry, snowberry, strawberry, sumac.

## SCRUB JAY
### APHELOCOMA COERULESCENS

**IDENTIFICATION:** 11 to 12½ inches (28-32 cm); large robin size; brown back, blue head, wings and tail, gray underparts, blue band on breast.

**NESTING:** 2 to 6 greenish eggs spotted brown in nest of oak twigs, in shrub or low tree.

**HABITAT:** brushland, foothills, oak-chaparral.

**RANGE:** breeds and winters in U.S. west from Wyoming and Texas.

**FEEDER FOODS:** (hanging, ground and suet feeders) black-stripe sunflower seeds, bread, corn, cracked nuts, peanut butter, suet.

**ATTRACTIVE PLANTINGS:** fir, juniper, pine.

## SONG SPARROW
MELOSPIZA MELODIA

**IDENTIFICATION:** 5 to 7 inches (13-17 cm); sparrow size; brown spotted or streaked black above, brown and gray head, gray below streaked black.

**NESTING:** 3 to 5 green eggs spotted brown in cup of grass and leaves lined with hair, on ground or in low shrub.

**HABITAT:** city parks, pastures, residential areas, thickets.

**RANGE:** breeds from southern Alaska to Newfoundland south through California and New Mexico, Kansas and South Carolina; winters south of the U.S.-Canadian border.

**FEEDER FOODS:** (suet and ground feeder) black-stripe sunflower seeds, cracked corn, hemp, peanut butter, suet, white proso millet.

**ATTRACTIVE PLANTINGS:** (thickets) amaranth, bachelor's buttons, blackberry, cosmos, mulberry, phlox, pine, poppy, viburnum, zinnia.

## TREE SPARROW
SPIZELLA ARBOREA

**IDENTIFICATION:** 5½ to 6½ inches (14-16 cm); sparrow size; streaked brown above, gray below, black spot in center of breast, gray head, brown crown, black ear stripe.

**NESTING:** 4 or 5 blue eggs spotted brown in cup of weed stems and bark strips lined with hair, near ground, in tundra.

**HABITAT:** summer, Arctic; winters in residential areas, thickets, woodland edge.

**RANGE:** breeds from northern Manitoba and Quebec south to central Manitoba and Quebec; winters south of the U.S.-Canadian border.

**FEEDER FOODS:** (ground feeder) black-stripe sunflower seeds, cracked corn, peanut hearts, white proso millet.

**ATTRACTIVE PLANTINGS:** (thickets).

## TREE SWALLOW
IRIDOPROCNE BICOLOR

**IDENTIFICATION:** 5 to 6¼ inches (13-16 cm); sparrow size; shimmering green-blue above, white below.

**NESTING:** 3 to 6 white eggs in a cup of feathers, in cavity.

**HABITAT:** open areas near water.

**RANGE:** breeds from northern Manitoba and Newfoundland south to Maryland and Nebraska; winters in southeast U.S.

**FEEDER FOODS:**–

**ATTRACTIVE PLANTINGS:** lawn.

## TUFTED TITMOUSE
PARUS BICOLOR

**IDENTIFICATION:** 5 to 6 inches (13-15 cm); sparrow size; gray above, white below, rust sides, gray crest.

**NESTING:** 4 to 8 white eggs speckled brown in cup of leaves and moss, in cavity.

**HABITAT:** swampy woodland, winters in residential areas.

**RANGE:** breeds and winters south of the U.S.-Canadian border, west of Minnesota, Nebraska and Texas.

**FEEDER FOODS:** (hanging, ground and suet feeders) black-stripe sunflower seeds, bread, crumbled doughnuts, nut meats, peanut kernels, raisins, suet.

**ATTRACTIVE PLANTINGS:** beech, blueberry, elderberry, hackberry, mulberry, oak, pine, strawberry, sweet birch, wax myrtle.

## WHITE-BREASTED NUTHATCH

SITTA CAROLINENSIS

**IDENTIFICATION:** 5 to 6 inches (13-15 cm); sparrow size; blue-gray above, white below, white face, black crown.

**NESTING:** 5 to 10 white eggs speckled brown in cup of grass and twigs lined with hair and soft grass, in cavity.

**HABITAT:** mixed forest.

**RANGE:** breeds and winters from Ontario and Nova Scotia south through the Gulf Coast.

**FEEDER FOODS:** (hanging, pole and suet feeders) crumbled doughnuts, nut meats, peanut butter, pumpkin and squash seeds, raw ground beef, suet, sunflower seeds.

**ATTRACTIVE PLANTINGS:** (large shade trees) beech, fir, hemlock, hickory, maple, oak, pine, spruce.

## WHITE-CROWNED SPARROW

ZONOTRICHIA LEUCOPHRYS

**IDENTIFICATION:** 6 to 7½ inches (15-19 cm); sparrow size; streaked brown and black above, gray below, sharply striped black and white crown.

**NESTING:** 3 to 5 pale green eggs spotted brown in cup of bark, twigs and grass lined with hair and soft grass, on or near ground.

**HABITAT:** dense brush near open grassland; winters in residential areas.

**RANGE:** breeds across northern Canada; winters from Mid-Atlantic U.S. south through Gulf Coast.

**FEEDER FOODS:** (ground feeder) black-stripe sunflower seeds, bread, cracked corn, hulled sunflower seeds, nut meats, white proso millet.

**ATTRACTIVE PLANTINGS:** amaranth, forget-me-not, phlox, poppy, zinnia.

## WHITE-THROATED SPARROW

ZONOTRICHIA ALBICOLLIS

**IDENTIFICATION:** 6 to 7 inches (15-18 cm); sparrow size; streaked brown and black above, gray below, striped black and white head, white throat, dark bill.

**NESTING:** 3 to 5 pale green eggs spotted brown in cup of grass and moss, on or near ground in undergrowth.

**HABITAT:** woodlands, winters in pastures and residential areas.

**RANGE:** breeds from southern Northwest Territories and north central Quebec south into the Great Lakes region of the U.S. and New England; winters from southern New York and the Great Lakes region south through the Gulf Coast.

**FEEDER FOODS:** (ground feeder) cracked corn, hulled sunflower seeds, peanut hearts, white proso millet.

**ATTRACTIVE PLANTINGS:** (hedgerows, thickets) phlox, zinnia.

## WOOD THRUSH

HYLOCICHLA MUSTELINA

**IDENTIFICATION:** 8 inches (20 cm); small robin size; brown above, white below spotted black, rust head.

**NESTING:** 3 or 4 blue-green eggs in cup of twigs and mud lined with soft grass, in shrub or small tree.

**HABITAT:** deciduous woodlands, parks, residential areas.

**RANGE:** breeds from southern Ontario and Quebec south throughout eastern half of U.S.; winters south of U.S.-Mexican border.

**FEEDER FOODS:** (ground feeder) corn meal.

**ATTRACTIVE PLANTINGS:** buckthorn, cherry, dogwood, holly, honeysuckle, huckleberry, rose, serviceberry, strawberry, viburnum, Virginia creeper.

·····················
## YELLOW WARBLER
DENDROICA PETECHIA
·····················

**IDENTIFICATION:** 4½ to 5 inches (11-13 cm); smaller than sparrow; bright yellow with light olive tinge on back; male, rust streaks on breast.

**NESTING:** 3 to 6 gray-white or blue-white eggs spotted brown in cup of bark and plant fibers lined with plant down and hair in fork of sapling.

**HABITAT:** residential areas, thickets.

**RANGE:** breeds from Alaska and northern Quebec south through U.S.; winters in the tropics.

**FEEDER FOODS:**—

**ATTRACTIVE PLANTINGS:** elm, Virginia creeper.

# Further reading

The following are selected books that have helped me in watching, identifying and attracting birds, and brought me to a greater understanding of the avian world:

Arbib, Robert and Tony Soper: *The Hungry Bird Book*, BALLANTINE BOOKS INC., NEW YORK, N. Y., 1965.

Armstrong, Edward A.: *The Ethology of Bird Display and Bird Behavior*, DOVER PUBLICATIONS INC., NEW YORK, N. Y., 1965.

Baines, Chris: *How to Make a Wildlife Garden*, ELM TREE BOOKS, LONDON, 1985.

Brainerd, John W.: *The Nature Observer's Handbook*, THE GLOBE PEQUOT PRESS, CHESTER, CONN., 1986.

Brainerd, John W.: *Working with Nature: A Practical Guide*, OXFORD UNIVERSITY PRESS INC., NEW YORK, N. Y., 1973.

Brown, Vinson: *The Amateur Naturalist's Handbook*, PRENTICE-HALL INC., ENGLEWOOD CLIFFS, N. J., 1980.

Bull, John and John Farrand, Jr.: *The Audubon Society Field Guide to North American Birds, Eastern Region*, ALFRED A. KNOPF, NEW YORK, N. Y., 1977.

Calkins, Carroll: *Gardening with Water, Plantings and Stone*, CORNERSTONE LIBRARY PUBLICATIONS, NEW YORK, N. Y., 1974.

Collins, Henry Hill: *Harper & Row's Complete Field Guide to North American Wildlife, Eastern Edition*, HARPER & ROW PUBLISHERS INC., NEW YORK, N. Y., 1981.

Collins, Henry Hill Jr., and Ned R. Boyajian: *Familiar Garden Birds of America*, HARPER & ROW, NEW YORK, N. Y., 1965.

Dennis, John V.: *Beyond the Bird Feeder*, ALFRED A. KNOPF, NEW YORK, N. Y., 1981.

Dennis, John V.: *The Wildlife Gardener*, ALFRED A. KNOPF, NEW YORK, N. Y., 1985.

Ehrlich, Paul R., David S. Dobkin and Darryl Wheye: *The Birder's Handbook*, SIMON & SCHUSTER INC., NEW YORK, N. Y., 1988.

Garber, Steven D.: *The Urban Naturalist*, JOHN WILEY & SONS INC., NEW YORK, N.Y., 1987.

Gellner, Sherry, ed.: *Attracting Birds to Your Garden*, LANE MAGAZINE AND BOOK COMPANY, MENLO PARK, CALIF., 1974.

Gillespie, John, ed.: *Garden Pools, Fountains and Waterfalls*, LANE PUBLISHING CO., MENLO PARK, CALIF., 1974.

Heintzelman, Donald S.: *A Manual for Bird Watching in the Americas*, UNIVERSE BOOKS, NEW YORK, N. Y., 1979.

Heintzelman, Donald S.: *The Birdwatcher's Activity Book*, STACKPOLE BOOKS, HARRISBURG, PA., 1983.

Harrison, Colin A.: *A Field Guide to the Nests, Eggs and Nestlings of North American Birds*, WILLIAM COLLINS PUBLISHERS INC., NEW YORK, N. Y., 1978.

Harrison, George: *The Backyard Bird Watcher,* SIMON & SCHUSTER INC., NEW YORK, N. Y., 1979.

Harrison, Hal H.: *A Field Guide to Birds' Nests,* HOUGHTON MIFFLIN CO., BOSTON, MASS., 1975.

Harrison, Kit and George: *America's Favorite Backyard Birds,* SIMON & SCHUSTER INC., NEW YORK, N. Y.,1983.

Kress, Stephen W.: *The Audubon Society Handbook for Birders,* CHARLES SCRIBNER'S SONS, NEW YORK, N. Y., 1981.

Kress, Stephen W.: *The Audubon Society Guide to Attracting Birds,* CHARLES SCRIBNER'S SONS, NEW YORK, N. Y., 1985.

Leahy, Christopher: *The Birdwatcher's Companion: An Encyclopedic Handbook of North American Birdlife,* HILL AND WANG, NEW YORK, N. Y., 1982.

Lemmon, Robert S.: *How to Attract the Birds,* DOUBLEDAY & CO. INC., NEW YORK, N. Y., 1947.

Levin, Ted: *Backtracking: The Way of a Naturalist,* CHELSEA GREEN PUBLISHING CO., CHELSEA, VT., 1987.

Logsdon, Gene: *Wildlife in Your Garden: or Dealing with Deer, Rabbits, Raccoons, Moles, Crows, Sparrows and Other of Nature's Creatures in Ways That Keep Them Around But Away from Your Fruits and Vegetables,* RODALE PRESS, EMMAUS, PA., 1983.

Luttringer, Leo A., Jr.: *Pennsylvania Birdlife,* PENNSYLVANIA GAME COMMISSION, HARRISBURG, PA., 1966.

Mahnken, Jan: *Feeding the Birds,* GARDEN WAY PUBLISHING, POWNAL, VT., 1983.

Margolin, Malcolm: *The Earth Manual,* HEYDAY BOOKS, BERKELEY, CALIF., 1975.

McKenney, Margaret: *Birds in the Garden: And How to Attract Them,* GROSSET & DUNLAP, NEW YORK, N. Y., 1939.

Palmer, Laurence: *Fieldbook of Natural History* (second edition), MCGRAW-HILL BOOK CO., NEW YORK, N. Y., 1975.

Perry, Francis: *The Water Garden,* VAN NOSTRAND REINHOLD CO., NEW YORK, N. Y., 1981.

Peterson, Roger Tory, ed.: *A Field Guide to the Birds,* HOUGHTON MIFFLIN CO., BOSTON, MASS., 1980.

Pettingill, Olin Sewall, Jr.: *A Guide to Bird Finding, East of the Mississippi* (second edition), HOUGHTON MIFFLIN CO., BOSTON, MASS., 1977.

Ransom, Jay Ellis: *Harper & Row's Complete Field Guide to North American Wildlife, Western Edition,* HARPER & ROW PUBLISHERS, NEW YORK, N. Y., 1981.

Robinson, Howard F., et al: *Planting an Oasis for Wildlife,* NATIONAL WILDLIFE FEDERATION, WASHINGTON, D. C., 1986.

Roth, Charles E.: *The Wildlife Observer's Guidebook,* PRENTICE-HALL INC., ENGLEWOOD CLIFFS, N. J., 1982.

Simonds, Calvin: *Private Lives of Garden Birds,* RODALE PRESS, EMMAUS, PA., 1983.

Stokes, Donald: *A Guide to Bird Behavior* (volume I), LITTLE, BROWN AND CO., BOSTON, MASS., 1979.

Stokes, Donald and Lillian: *A Guide to Bird Behavior* (volume II), LITTLE, BROWN AND CO., BOSTON, MASS., 1983.

Stokes, Donald and Lillian: *The Bird Feeder Book,* LITTLE, BROWN AND CO., BOSTON, MASS., 1987.

Teale, Edwin Way: *A Naturalist Buys an Old Farm,* DODD, MEAD & CO., NEW YORK, N. Y., 1974.

Terres, John K.: *Songbirds in Your Garden,* THOMAS Y. CROWELL CO., NEW YORK, N. Y., 1968.

Terres, John K.: *The Audubon Society Encyclopedia of North American Birds,* ALFRED A. KNOPF, NEW YORK, N. Y., 1980.

Tufts, Craig: *The Backyard Naturalist,* NATIONAL WILDLIFE FEDERATION, WASHINGTON, D. C., 1988.

Welty, John Carl: *The Life of Birds,* W. B. SAUNDERS CO., PHILADELPHIA, PA., 1962.

Wetmore, Alexander, et al: *Song and Garden Birds of North America,* NATIONAL GEOGRAPHIC SOCIETY, WASHINGTON, D. C., 1964.

A few books that have helped my photography to the point that it is now appearing in magazines and books such as this one are the following:

Angel, Heather: *Nature Photography: Its art and techniques,* FOUNTAIN PRESS, LONDON, 1972.

Bennett, Edna: *Nature Photography Simplified,* THE AMERICAN PHOTOGRAPHIC BOOK PUBLISHING CO. INC., NEW YORK, N. Y., 1975.

Hedgecoe, John: *Pocket Guide to Practical Photography,* SIMON & SCHUSTER INC., NEW YORK, N. Y., 1979.

Kreh, Left: *The L. L. Bean Guide to Outdoor Photography,* RANDOM HOUSE, NEW YORK, N. Y., 1988.

McDonald, Joe: *A Practical Guide to Photographing American Wildlife,* FOXY-OWL PUBLICATIONS, WHITEHALL, PA., 1983.

Shaw, John: *The Nature Photographer's Complete Guide to Professional Field Techniques,* WATSON-GUPTILL PUBLICATIONS, NEW YORK, N. Y., 1984.

# Index

# Acknowledgments

KEY: *t* = top; *b* = bottom; *l* = left; *r* = right; *c* = centre; *m* = main picture; *i* = inset

© Richard Day: PAGES 17, 27, 82, 83, 96 *r*. © Kerry A Grim: PAGES 28, 58 *t*, 71 *r*. © Joe McDonald: PAGES 9, 11, 15 *r*, 31, 32, 34/5, 38, 40/1, 46, 47, 61, 77, 78/9, 84 *l*, 92 *cl r*, 96 *cr*, 97 *cl*, 100 *cl*, 101 *cl r*, 102 *l*, 103 *cl*, 106 *cl cr*. © Doris Palmer Wilson: PAGE 21. © Leonard Lee Rue III: PAGES 10 *b*, 12, 14 *t*, 18, 22, 23, 24 *m*, 50, 52, 74, 97 *r*. © Len Rue Jr: PAGES 25, 48/9, 81. © Marcus Schneck: PAGES 8, 10 *t*, 15 *l*, 16 *t b*, 19 *r*, 26 *l*, 33, 37, 41 *r*, 44, 45, 49 *tr br*, 58 *b*, 68/9, 70/1, 72 *t b*, 73, 80, 104 *l*. © Gregory K Scott: PAGES 6, 26 *m*, 42, 57 *r*, 88, 94 *r*, 96 *cl*, 98/9. © VIREO – S Bahrt: PAGE 64/5; H Clarke: PAGES 94 *cl*, 95 *cr*; H Cruickshank: PAGES 93 *r*, 106 *r*; W Greene: PAGES 93 *cl*, 94 *l*; C H Greenwalt: PAGES 92 *cr*, 93 *l*, 94 *cr*, 95 *r*, 97 *cr*, 104 *cl*; Steven Holt: PAGES 93 *cr*, 101 *cr*; S J Lang: PAGE 104 *cr*; C R Sams II & J F Stoick: PAGE 103 *r*; P K Schleicher: PAGES 100 *cr*, 105 *cr*, B Schorre: PAGES 30, 102 *cl*, 107 *l*; R Villens: PAGE 101 *l*; J R Woodward: PAGES 36, 56, 92 *l*, 95 *cl*, 96 *l*, 97 *l*, 100 *l*, 102 *cr r*, 103 *cr*, 105 *l cl*, 105 *r*, 108 *l*; D & M Zimmerman: PAGES 95 *l*, 104 *r*; © Scott Weidensaul: PAGES 19 *l*, 20, 24 *l*, 53, 54 *m l*, 57 *l*, 59, 60, 66, 84/5, 86/7, 90, 101 *r*, 103 *l*.

With special thanks to Jill Caravan and Scott Weidensaul.